C000245648

Photo by Joan Marcus

A scene from the New York production of *The Temperamentals.* From left to right: Michael Urie, Arnie Burton, Sam Breslin Wright, Matthew Schneck, and Thomas Jay Ryan.

THE TEMPERAMENTALS

BY JON MARANS

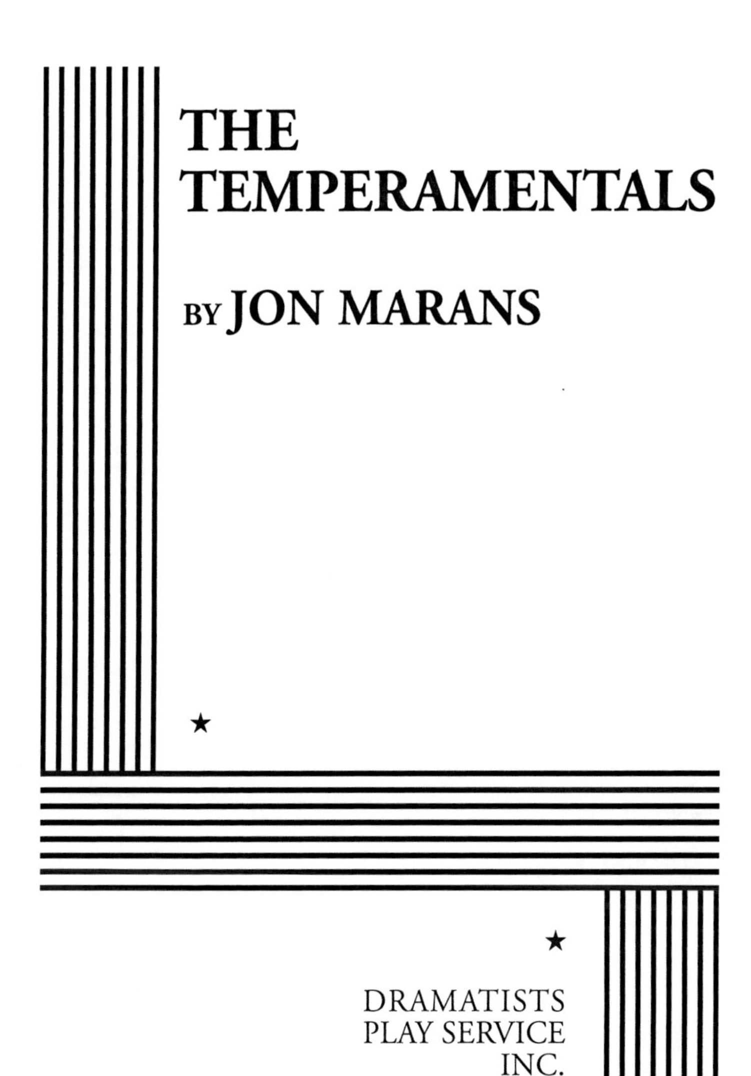

DRAMATISTS
PLAY SERVICE
INC.

This play is dedicated to the original
Mattachine visionaries

and to

Daryl Roth
Jonathan Silverstein
Kevin McAnarney
and
Stacy Shane

AUTHOR'S NOTE

While this isn't a musical, certain musical elements greatly help the storytelling. Therefore, it's vital for MAN #1 to play the ukulele. Fortunately, it's a fairly easy instrument to learn and only eight chords are used throughout the entire play.

It would also be terrific for MAN #2 to play the clarinet. However, that instrument is difficult to learn. If MAN #2 isn't already proficient at the clarinet, it might make more sense for him to mime playing it to pre-recorded music. (The clarinet sheet music is included in the back of this script.) The other possibility is for MAN #2 to learn the recorder and perhaps play some of the pieces live — particularly "Nelly Queens." And then have the rest of the music pre-recorded and mime playing them. (Obviously the recorder gives a less elegant sound than the clarinet.)

On a much more personal note, writing about these five brave men was not only a labor of love, but an eye-opening exploration of a world that was relatively unknown to me. For those who find these men and this subject matter equally absorbing, I urge you to read Stuart Timmons' book *The Trouble with Harry Hay* (Alyson Publications).

THE TEMPERAMENTALS was produced by Daryl Roth, Stacy Shane and Martian Entertainment at New World Stages in New York City, performances beginning on February 18th, 2010. The associate producer was Alexander Fraser. The general manager was Adam Hess; the company manager was Kyle Provost. It was directed by Jonathan Silverstein; set and costume designs were by Clint Ramos; lighting design by Josh Bradford; sound design by Daniel Kluger; graphic design by Adrian Sie; casting by Stephanie Klapper. The production stage manager was Tom Taylor; assistant stage manager was Julie DeRossi. The media co-ordinator was Thomas Dooley. The press rep was Kevin P. McAnarney. The cast was as follows:

HARRY HAY .... Thomas Jay Ryan
RUDI GERNREICH .... Michael Urie
CHUCK ROWLAND & others .... Arnie Burton
BOB HULL & others .... Matthew Schneck
DALE JENNINGS & others .... Sam Breslin Wright

THE TEMPERAMENTALS was originally produced in New York City by Stacy Shane and premiered at the Barrow Group Studio Theater in New York on April 30th, 2009. It moved to the TBG Theater in New York City on June 10th, 2009, produced by Daryl Roth and Stacy Shane. It was directed by Jonathan Silverstein; set and costume designs were by Clint Ramos; lighting design by Josh Bradford; sound design by Daniel Kluger. Porter Pickard was the company manager; Adrian Sie was the graphic designer. The production stage manager was Samone B. Weissman and the assistant stage manager was Paloma Pilar. Kevin P. McAnarney was the press rep. The cast was as follows:

HARRY HAY .... Thomas Jay Ryan
RUDI GERNREICH .... Michael Urie
CHUCK ROWLAND & others .... Tom Beckett
BOB HULL & others .... Matthew Schneck
DALE JENNINGS & others .... Sam Breslin Wright

CHARACTERS

HARRY HAY

RUDI GERNREICH (who also plays WOMAN #4)

Man #1:

CHUCK ROWLAND

VINCENTE

WOMAN #2 and others

plays ukulele

Man #2:

BOB HULL

GEORGE SHIBLEY

WOMAN #1 and others

plays clarinet (or recorder)

Man #3:

DALE JENNINGS

NIGEL BUTLER

WOMAN #3 and others

SETTING

THE TEMPERAMENTALS takes place in the early 1950s in various locations throughout Los Angeles.

As the play is in many different locales, the set should not be realistic. Instead, each locale only need supply us with atmosphere. Most of the settings are secluded, out-of-the-way places. Where secrecy can not only grow but thrive — in a heady, intoxicating way. Where a secret language hangs in the air — much more vibrant and alive than the English language that all of these characters speak.

Anyone who looks at something special, in a very original way, makes you see it that way forever.

—George Cukor

THE TEMPERAMENTALS

ACT ONE

Late at night. The Chuckwagon Diner.

1950. It appears *we're in a small hole-in-the-wall restaurant in the Wild West.*

Actually, we're in an L.A. restaurant.

Two men in suits sit across from each other at a table: Rudi and Harry. Rudi is 29, pale, interestingly handsome, wildly charming. Harry is 39, pushy, gruff, blustery, and imperious. Rudi speaks with just a trace of a Viennese accent.

Perhaps in the shadows, a menacing man also in a suit watches on. Imminent danger must always hang over Rudi and Harry whether or not the danger is actually present.

Harry stares out for a couple of seconds. The silence rings out and then:

HARRY. It really IS like a cameo.
RUDI. *(Amused.)* … Well … hmmm … what can I say.
HARRY. Like the face of an ancient Greek woman. *(Off Rudi's annoyed glare.)* OR man … Majestic. Regal. Unreachable.
RUDI. Now, truly, what can I say?
HARRY. You don't know what cameo means — do you? Don't sweat it.
RUDI. *(Amused.)* I would hardly be sweating. I'd simply ask you. *(Harry slowly puts his foot on top of Rudi's. Rudi startles.)* Ah! Your

foot, Harry.
HARRY. What?
RUDI. Is on top of mine.
HARRY. And therefore protecting you.
RUDI. Almost crushing me.
HARRY. Should I stop?
RUDI. Don't be ridiculous. I said "almost." *(Beat.)*
HARRY. *(Testing him.)* So what DOES the word "cameo" mean?
RUDI. It's a kind of engraving on a stone. And as you chip away to carve the face, you find another color exists. The underlying color of the stone.
HARRY. *(Stunned, but trying to hide it.)* Correct.
RUDI. You didn't remotely know that.
HARRY. Correct again. How did you figure that out?
RUDI. Your foot relaxed. *(Harry's amused.)*
HARRY. So most stones have a second color?
RUDI. Of course. But which is the true color? The inner or the outer?
HARRY. The inner, of course.
RUDI. Yes. Perhaps. Although who says a stone can only have one true color? Why not two?
HARRY. I keep forgetting.
RUDI. What?
HARRY. That you were born in Vienna. *(Rudi looks puzzled.)* Raised on art, culture.
RUDI. *(Amused.)* Just because I'm from … I promise you, Vienna has its share of stupid people. A famous saying: "After all the Jews had fled or been killed — and then after the war when all the Nazis went into hiding — nothing was left in Vienna except for — the unexceptional."
HARRY. And look at that. You put yourself into one of the exceptional categories.
RUDI. The quotation did that for me.
HARRY. However it failed to mention —
RUDI. Yes?
HARRY. The Temperamentals. Also persecuted. Equally exceptional.
RUDI. Although they would hardly be part of the saying.
HARRY. Not yet. But someday they'll — *(A glass breaks offstage or a man clears his throat. Harry and Rudi are instantly on alert — as if a gun just went off. Harry cautiously looks over to see what happened.*

Rudi doesn't turn. Then Harry stares at Rudi — communicating in the silence that everything is fine. Their conversation picks up where it left off.) Someday the Temperamentals will not only be *making* the quotes, but be *in* them.
RUDI. *(Amused.)* It seems highly unlikely that civilized conversations would include people who are —
HARRY. *(Firmly.)* I guarantee it will happen. I guarantee it. Because of me. *(There is something about Harry's strength that Rudi finds strangely appealing.)*
RUDI. *(Tickled.)* Because of you?
HARRY. *(Getting louder as he speaks.)* I was born on Easter Sunday. The *Titanic* went down the following Thursday. And why? Two *Titanic*s can't exist in the world at one time! When one shows up, the other *has* to go down!
RUDI. Harry.
HARRY. Yes, Rudi.
RUDI. Please, modulate your voice.
HARRY. At the Chuckwagon Diner?! … I wasn't saying anything inappropriate.
RUDI. No, but when you get excited you talk … loudly. And spit. *(Harry is stunned that Rudi said that.)*
HARRY. I'll try to be more aware of those things.
RUDI. A cameo is also a word in *my* business. The motion picture business.
HARRY. *Your* business? *(Harry chuckles.)*
RUDI. You're amused?
HARRY. Well … aren't you an *assistant* costume designer or something like that?
RUDI. Now *that's* amusing. I must tell that joke to all of my assistant designers … *(Throwing it away.)* And Lana Turner.
HARRY. … You've designed for — ? *(Rudi nods nonchalantly.)* … Sorry. I just assumed — I mean all the other young artsy types that I've … known —
RUDI. *(Amused.)* All the *other* young — ? … So what is a cameo — in *my* business? If you're unsure, please don't be afraid to ask —
HARRY. It's a small, but pivotal role played by a somewhat well-known actor — or actress. Usually just one scene.
RUDI. *(Trying to be matter-of-fact.)* Yes.
HARRY. Now you're the one who's stunned!
RUDI. Correct.

HARRY. I used to be an actor before I began — *(With a mystery to it.)* teaching. *(Harry stares at Rudi. Wondering. Then from under the table, Harry lifts up an old battered briefcase, takes out a few sheets of paper, hands it to Rudi.)*
RUDI. Why are you —
HARRY. Read it.
RUDI. But what exactly —
HARRY. *(Firmly, although quite anxious underneath.)* I said "Read it!" *(As Rudi begins to look it over, Harry speaks.)* Last week — after we met, I thought — sure we disagreed about the war, but at least we were both *in* the argument. Although I still say, you can't go into a country uninvited —
RUDI. Helping them is the *right* thing to do.
HARRY. *(Loving the fight.)* Can't help every country in trouble, dammit.
RUDI. *(Personal.)* Or people. And certainly didn't. As my entire family could attest to.
HARRY. THAT was obviously horrible —
RUDI. And today's situation in Asia is equally volatile —
HARRY. We can't get involved in someone else's war —
RUDI. For the bigger picture, we must! And will. Because whatever the president says when it comes to national security, the country accepts.
HARRY. They do not.
RUDI. You're being naïve.
HARRY. *(Pissed off.)* You're being Viennese. *(They stare at each other for a moment. It's a standoff.)* Nothing like a good argument to get the blood going.
RUDI. *(Turned on.)* Mine is certainly racing. *(As Rudi continues looking at the document, he is so stunned by what he reads that he puts his hand on Harry's arm. Which makes Harry uneasy. Even more so if a man in the shadows steps out, glaring at this inappropriate behavior.)*
HARRY. Rudi, your hand.
RUDI. After what I've seen in Vienna, I don't care. From what you have written, I think neither do you. *(Harry takes Rudi's hand and removes it from his arm.)*
HARRY. People have been arrested for less than that.
RUDI. I intend to continue doing it. You need to get used to it. Do not disappoint me next time. *(Rudi continues reading.)*
HARRY. *(Pleased by Rudi's pluck.)* Your face.

RUDI. Yes?
HARRY. *(Smitten.)* It really *is* like a cameo.
RUDI. This document —
HARRY. Yes?
RUDI. — is the most dangerous thing I have ever seen … Count me in. *(Blackout. As the men remove their clothing, lights slowly up on an attic-like room where it's difficult to stand, especially on the sides. Harry sits, barefoot. While an oddly subservient Rudi — shirtless — is in the middle of putting on Harry's socks. As he does, Harry looks at a sketchbook.)* Excuse me, but that is private.
HARRY. And putting my socks on isn't? *(Rudi continues putting socks on.)* What IS this design?
RUDI. A houndstooth check.
HARRY. *(Looking at design.)* They're so damn large.
RUDI. When I create, I believe in making bold statements.
HARRY. *That* — I approve of.
RUDI. However, the actual pattern is simple and elegant. So it's a bold statement — but on a classic pattern.
HARRY. *(Looking at sketchbook, a dress pattern.)* A bold statement on a classic pattern.
RUDI. That I believe everyone can wear.
HARRY. *(Correcting him.)* Every *woman* can wear.
RUDI. Why not men as well? All of them swapping and sharing the clothes I design. *(Harry, slightly amused, laughs. Rudi glares.)* Did I laugh at your manifesto?
HARRY. … No.
RUDI. I also try to give myself dilemmas — to challenge myself. Can I make a dress out of a simple geometric shape? *(Rudi pulls a long black gown out of a bag. Holds it up.)* It looks like an ordinary gown. Although incredibly stylish. I particularly like the way the satin and the matte silk compliment each other while both being black. But I digress. It looks like an ordinary gown. But — *(Rudi lays the gown down on the ground. The actual shape is a huge circle.)* The dress is actually one incredibly large —
HARRY. *(Stunned.)* — Circle. Damn.
RUDI. *(Pulling out a small cape from the bag that matches the gown.)* Even the cape —
HARRY. — Is a circle.
RUDI. Next, I will design a gown from a square. *(Rudi holds out the cape to Harry.)* Put it on. You'll also see how comfortable it feels.

(Harry won't.) Go on … *(Harry looks at it. Tempted.)* I know you want to. *(But Harry won't. Rudi grabs it and puts it on himself. Displays it. This makes Harry uncomfortable.)*
HARRY. *(Changing subject.)* Rudi? Your shirt.
RUDI. Hmmm?
HARRY. *(Ordering him.)* Put it back on. *(As Rudi puts his shirt back on, Harry returns to a previous subject.)* So our document. Two years ago, I tried to get some people onboard. No success. So this time I've decided to —
RUDI. *(Interrupting.)* Stop. You're jumping ahead.
HARRY. To the solution.
RUDI. First, what went wrong?
HARRY. You don't need to bother yourself with all that.
RUDI. If I am to be part of this mission, I do.
HARRY. I already have an answer.
RUDI. *(Abrupt.)* Without my participation? Then I do not care to hear this brilliant solution. Or be a part of "your" dream. *(Beat. Harry is shaken. And puzzled.)*
HARRY. Rudi?
RUDI. Yes.
HARRY. *(Commanding, still into the sex-play.)* Put my shoes on.
RUDI. That part's over. Start from the beginning. *(They stare at each other. Aware of the impasse. Finally …)*
HARRY. August 10th, 1948. Westlake Park.
RUDI. The park?
HARRY. Where I met Paul Fal — *(Stops himself. Doesn't want to say the man's last name.)* Paul. Who invited me to a beer blast with about twelve men.
RUDI. A — "sophisticated" jury?
HARRY. More like a hanging one. *(Two men enter, standing in the shadows, talking. Harry steps into their scene.)* The minute I walked in — *(The two men immediately lower their voices. Turn away from Harry. Harry stares at each one. Each turns away. Harry turns back to Rudi.)* For the first time in my life, I suddenly became reticent to speak.
RUDI. *(Amazed.)* You?!
HARRY. I leaned against the wall — tried to listen — for clues.
RUDI. Clues?
HARRY. On how to, well, fit in.
RUDI *(Understands how difficult that can be.)* Yes. So you put up — "the mask"?

HARRY. Until someone mentioned Henry Wallace. Then it came crashing down. *(Jumping into the middle of that conversation.)* With someone as progressive as Wallace running for president, I think change is finally possible.
MAN #1. *(The meeker of the two.)* No one's debating that … *(Softly.)* here.
HARRY. No?
MAN #1. No.
HARRY. *(Getting an idea.)* Then how 'bout our organization being represented at the Democratic Convention under the wing of Henry Wallace and the Progressive Party! We'll call ourselves "Bachelors for Wallace!"
MAN #2. How much beer have you had? "Bachelors for" — ? … And no one here said we were an organization. We're just a beer blast!
HARRY. *(Annoyed.)* Who the hell are you kidding?!
MAN #1. No one. Because for the record, none us here are — "that way."
MAN #2. *(Accusatory to Harry.)* But are you? *(They wait for his answer, unsure if Harry's a spy infiltrating their group.)*
HARRY. *(Firmly.)* My family are Mayflower descendants. Have always understood risk, revolution, AND — entitlement. When the authorities tried to take my ancestors' rights away, they stood up. Now — when MY rights are being taken away —
MAN #2. *(Stunned he outed himself.) Your* rights?
HARRY. Yes. My rights. Which is why we have to organize.
MAN #2. *(Tentatively.)* … No disagreement here.
HARRY. Good. But first we need: *(Harry finds a sheet of paper.)* A Declaration of Independence. *(Man #1 takes a pen out of his pocket and ceremoniously holds it out to Harry. It's all slightly silly and deeply earnest at the same time. Harry takes the pen. To Rudi.)* And so I began to write. And by the end of that evening had finished the first draft of that manifesto I showed you. *(Man #1 grabs the piece of paper. Man #1 and Man #2 read it — stunned. Moved. Then nervous.)*
RUDI. *(Surprised.)* In front of them?
HARRY. They goaded me into it. Besides, I rise to a challenge … As I wrote, I realized that my true destiny was finally beginning … However, the next day I phoned up the guys who had shown such enthusiasm the night before. My bubble promptly burst in the dawn's early light. All of them — scared.

MAN #2. *(Exiting with Man #1.)* That was just the beer talking!
HARRY. Like little girls. No, sissies!
RUDI. … So for the last two years, no one has wanted to get near your crazy dream.
HARRY. No. *(Rudi kneels, helping Harry put on his shoes.)* I thought that part was over?
RUDI. I'll need sixty copies of your treatise. But this time, it'll go to more viable people.
HARRY. Viable?
RUDI. Connected. Social. Bright young people.
HARRY. *(Attitude.)* Your circle.
RUDI. *Ja. Natürlich.*
HARRY. Communism teaches us it's the poor who change things.
RUDI. Open your eyes, Harry. This is the USA, not Russia. *(Rudi continues putting Harry's shoes on.)*
HARRY. What makes you think you can convince people when I can't?
RUDI. *(Amused.)* Oh, Harry … I — am charming. *(Suddenly an extremely loud bell chimes. Both men cover their ears.)* We MUST find another free place for these assignations. *(Re: this place.)* I mean, a clock tower. Of a Catholic church, no less.
HARRY. Well we can't just get a hotel. Two men. Sharing a room. In the middle of the day.
RUDI. Why not?
HARRY. I can't believe it's already two o'clock … I have to get back to class. *(Harry and Rudi continue dressing.)* Next week, I want you to arrive first and only wear —
RUDI. Harry.
HARRY. Yes, Rudi.
RUDI. Next time, could we — connect more?
HARRY. *(Puzzled.)* Connect?
RUDI. Be more romantic.
HARRY. Oh. Romantic. I didn't realize you liked — *(Never did it before.)* I'm sure I can do that.
RUDI. So am I. But for now, *I* must run.
HARRY. Lana Turner?
RUDI. *(Air of mystery.)* Edith Head. *(Rudi exits. Harry stands there, watching Rudi go. Intrigued by him. End scene. Lights shift as we hear cocktail music playing and people talking [Man #1 and Man #3]. It's evening at a swanky party. Harry tries to slip on a jacket*

which has the document folded in the inside pocket. A well-dressed Rudi has by now reentered and reaches over to help him. They look at each other with affection and then Harry — with the fear that someone may be looking — pulls away. Tries to fix the jacket himself. However, Rudi — used to helping people make clothes look right — reaches back over and fixes Harry's jacket.) Stop fidgeting.
HARRY. I can do it myself.
RUDI. Certainly not as well as I can. And almost done.
HARRY. Stop.
RUDI. This is Hollywood. People touch. I think the actors *(With disdain.)* … need it.
HARRY. Tonight, *we* need at least one person. Who do we have?
RUDI. You tell me. *(Harry looks around. It's Hollywood — they all seem light in the loafers.)*
HARRY. All of them. *(Looks again.)* None of them?
RUDI. Vincente. *(Rudi looks over to where a dapper-looking Vincente [Man #1] is standing.)*
HARRY. Vincente?! Damn … Are you sure? Vincente?!
RUDI. AND — I think we stand a chance.
HARRY. What a coup. It would shake the world.
RUDI. Especially his. Still, he's expecting us. And Harry.
HARRY. Yes, Rudi.
RUDI. Stand tall.
HARRY. Is my posture — ?
RUDI. He likes tall men. *(They start over.)*
HARRY. If Vincente turns us down, we should still —
RUDI. No! Do not ask about *her*.
HARRY. Her? … No, we should still go to the Chuckwagon and read through the papers. Argue about the news.
RUDI. Oh, right … If he says "no," I may not want to.
HARRY. That's why I'm bringing it up now.
RUDI. *(Watching Vincente, slipping into a word of French.) Attends.* Vincente wants out of his conversation!
HARRY. How can you tell?
RUDI. The way he keeps stepping back. Body language tells a lot.
HARRY. That other guy might just have lousy breath.
RUDI. No, Vincente wants out. *(Mimicking Harry's words.) I* guarantee it … Our chance has arrived.
HARRY. To?
RUDI. Be his savior. *(Quickly going over to Vincente and Other Man*

[played by Man #3], thinking fast, acting indignant.) And I tell you again, Vincente —
VINCENTE. *(Thrilled.)* Yes?
RUDI. I know Paris. After all, I *am* European. And street urchins simply do not dress with that much panache.
OTHER MAN. I'm in the middle of a story —
RUDI. *Ja. (Back to Vincente.)* They must be loose enough to dance in. But my sketches are more authentic. Look them over —
VINCENTE. *(Playing along with the game.)* I'm fairly set.
RUDI. It is vital to show some of the harsh, gritty reality —
VINCENTE. Next to Gene Kelly in his form-fitting costume?
RUDI. That is a problem as well.
VINCENTE. *(To Rudi.)* Now you're being ridiculous. *(To Other Man.)* I'm so sorry. Work.
OTHER MAN. *(Pissed off.)* Of course. *(As Other Man exits, mutters to himself.)* A gritty musical. *(Other Man exits.)*
VINCENTE. *(To Rudi.)* My hero. Although I don't recall hiring you for *An American in Paris.*
RUDI. I was reassigned. Today. To takeover all designs.
VINCENTE. Liar. Although someday, instead of "Costumes by Irene Sharaff" or "Edith Head"— "By Rudi!" It's just a matter of — *(Remembering.)* Hold on. I'm having a business luncheon next week. With quite a few directors attending. You must also be there so I can "specially" introduce you to them. *(Rudi is silent.)* You're supposed to say "thank you."
RUDI. And I do thank you.
VINCENTE. But?
RUDI. No, buts. I would love to put my stamp on a film. *However,* I have also been working on some dress designs. Not for a film. But for all women.
VICENTE. *(Seeing Rudi's drive.)* All women?
RUDI. So if you'd like to invite me to an intimate gathering with Elsa Schiaperelli. Or your friend Christian Dior —
VINCENTE. *(Surprised at his ballsiness.)* Christian Dior?
RUDI. — I could show them my "brilliant" designs. Which I promise you — will make *theirs* look so old-fashioned, they will instantly hire me. *(Vincente laughs. Rudi laughs along. Harry laughs louder, to be noticed.)* This is Harry. Whom I mentioned.
HARRY. I brought the manifesto. Got it right here in my pocket! *(Both Rudi and Vincente are a little surprised that Harry is so upfront*

and in your face. And loud. Especially on this dangerous subject matter. In public no less. But Harry just can't help himself. It's his personality.)
VINCENTE. It's much cooler in the garden. Have you seen the acacia tree out back?
RUDI. Not yet. *(Vincente guides them over there.)*
VINCENTE. Follow me. And don't get lost. *(To Harry.)* I've seen it.
HARRY. The acacia tree?
VINCENTE. *(He wasn't referring to that.)* Rudi was kind enough to show it to me. It's very bold.
HARRY. *(Catching on.)* Oh.
RUDI. *(Also understands Vincente.)* Without being impossible. Right?
VINCENTE. Rudi, you are so charming. It's difficult to say no to you. But eventually —
HARRY. No, no, you don't get it! You *gotta* do this. You are the ideal guy. Once married — to a star no less! Then divorced. Making you even *more* masculine. Woman after woman on your arm.
VINCENTE. In the public's eyes.
HARRY. Still, no one would doubt you love the ladies. So if you signed our manifesto, they'd just assume you believed in — humanitarian causes.
VINCENTE. What you say makes perfect sense … *before* 1947.
HARRY. Oh come on, the blacklist has only made our party stronger! And what I've learned as a member — has guided me every step of the way in writing this. *(Vincente is horrified to hear Harry talk about the Communist Party. And admit he's a member. Vincente walks them to a more secluded spot.)*
VINCENTE. Harry.
HARRY. Yes, Vincente.
VINCENTE. There are two subjects today one must never discuss in the open air. The first one, for fear of reprisal. The second, for fear of making it mundane … Consider: a woman forgets to put the stopper back on her favorite perfume. An indescribable scent fills the air. *(Re: Harry.)* Then soon becomes overpowering. Eventually, however, as the stopper remains off — the perfume is drained of all its aroma. And that ineffable scent, that unspeakably sophisticated, tart, tangy bouquet, is lost to the heavens.
HARRY. *(Both personal and political to Harry.)* Not lost. In the air. AND, a part of the air.
RUDI. And just like the rest of the air.
HARRY. *(Growing louder.)* No! Not just like the rest! Still different.

And unique. But embraced as one of the many scents that make up the air we breathe.
VINCENTE. You have twisted my story! … *(Impressed.)* Into a more inspirational one. You may be even more dangerous than Rudi.
HARRY. Good. So you'll sign this — ?
RUDI. *(Not wanting him to push too hard.)* Harry!
VINCENTE. Harry's a live wire. Be careful, Rudi.
HARRY. *(A one-track mind.)* So will you sign —
VINCENTE. *(Blurting out his fear.)* I am afraid … *(Covering.)* that *An American in Paris* — which I believe to be a historic film — will bomb even worse than *The Pirate.* The public isn't ready for it. *(Re: the manifesto.)* The public just isn't ready.
RUDI. You may surprise even yourself, Mr. Minnelli.
VINCENTE. *(Confiding.)* Look inside my mouth. *(Vincente opens his mouth. Rudi hesitates.)* Do it. *(Rudi does.)* See all the places I've bit on the inside. In this cheek. This one. Look way down here. *(To Harry.)* You can look as well.
HARRY. *(Doesn't want to look.)* I trust Rudi.
VINCENTE. Some actors have flop sweat when they go onstage. I don't sweat. I bite — the inside of my mouth — the entire time I'm filming a new movie. But I only bite on movies that end up being flops. Even if *I* think it'll be a hit, the mouth always knows the truth … And Harry, your "acacia tree" — is already causing my mouth to bleed. *(Vincente exits.)*
HARRY. *(Pissed off that they didn't get Vincente to sign.)* Just to annoy him, I SHOULD have asked about *her!* And I don't even like her … well … much.
RUDI. Harry.
HARRY. Yes, Rudi.
RUDI. He's right … You *were* inspirational. *(For a moment Rudi lets his hand graze against Harry. It's sweet and tender. Harry pulls away. Rudi glares at him. Then Harry remembers that Rudi expects them to touch in public. Harry looks around to see if anyone is looking. Slowly Harry moves closer to Rudi and finally lets his hand graze against Rudi's. There is an odd thrill as they not only express their affection, but realize the danger of it. And even get off on it. They continue nervously grazing their hands against each other until the end of the scene.)* There's no reason to be ashamed. *(Off Harry's puzzlement.)* … Of liking — "her."
HARRY. Oh, I'm not. It's just — the way guys go on. *(Imitating*

an effeminate guy.) "Did you see how she twisted her head when she sang — " *(Sings, from the song "Get Happy.")* "GET READY, GET READY" *(Spoken, imitating another Garland-obsessed gay guy.)* "Or the way she held that last note in the 'Trolley Song' and then the bells continued. Softer, but still driving. Heaven." Ugh. Their obsessiveness: it's embarrassing.

RUDI. *(Dryly.) I* agree. Same as guys talking about baseball all the time — *so* embarrassing. Right?

HARRY. No.

RUDI. But the way they go on about every move! *(Imitating a sports fanatic.)* "Didja see how the shortstop dove for the ball? And … caught it! Then twisted around, whipped the ball over to the first baseman. So smooth. That is the fifth time he's done it in nine games! Fifth time." … That's not obsessive?

HARRY. But not embarrassing.

RUDI. Because?

HARRY. That's what guys talk about. It's just the basic buzz —

RUDI. — that's in the air … So we accept it. Why can't our kind of talk *also* just be in the air? Why can't our babblings about Judy Garland be just as dull and annoying as their talk about baseball? *(Harry takes that in as they continue to lightly touch, each waiting for the other to pull away. To be the first to break. AND, to break away from the other.)*

HARRY. Vincente was wrong … You're the inspirational one. *(Rudi and Harry continue to touch. For now, they are together. Lights flash into the next scene. Rudi exits. To an offstage Rudi.)* Last night, 107 Gold Cup was packed. Not surprising. We got raided last Tuesday, so everyone assumed it'd be a couple of weeks before the cops came back. Still — whenever someone new came in, guys would cower in the corner. Cover our faces … Hardly the best atmosphere to find new recruits. But today we're going to round up hundreds. … So! — Our Temperamentals have made *two* beaches their own. The slice of Malibu between the pier and the spit — *and* the section below the Palisades just west of Marion Davies' waterfront estate. Which is your pleasure? *(Rudi enters in stylish swim trunks, holding petition and clipboard.)*

RUDI. *(As if there were no choice.)* The Marion Davies' estate, of course. *(Suddenly lights flood one side of the stage— blindingly bright. We're at the beach. Rudi holds out the petition, speaking to Man #3, also in trunks.)*

MAN #3. *(Very masculine, marine-like.)* Believe you me, this will not recall the troops we've sent to Korea. But … ah hell, I'll sign the damn thing. *(As Man #3 signs the Stockholm Petition.)*
RUDI. *(Testing the man.)* Nice bathing trunks. The pattern.
MAN #3. *(Looking him in the eye, masculine but flirtatious.)* Uh … Thanks … buddy.
RUDI. We're also having a meeting discussing *(Said softer.)* the Kinsey Report.
MAN #3. *(Thrown that Kinsey is said out loud.)* Really?
RUDI. The section about social deviancy. So if you'd like to attend, these are the particulars.
MAN #3. *(Tempted, but then gets defensive.)* You saying I'm a queer?
RUDI. Would that so terrible? *(Off Man #3's glare.)* Sorry. *(Lights crash down on them and up on the other beach with a fully clothed Harry and Man #2.)*
MAN #2. *(A professorial type, looking over petition.)* Wow. The Stockholm Petition. I heard DuBois — that guy who founded the N-Double-A-C-P — was arrested for circulating this.
HARRY. *(Already starting to take it from him and move on.)* Then don't sign it.
MAN #2. I didn't say that. This war is ridiculous. And once we get in, there's no end in sight. *(As Man #2 signs.)*
HARRY. Our organization is also holding a forum to discuss the Kinsey Report.
MAN #2. *(Stunned to hear Kinsey spoken.)* Good for you. *(Whispered.)* Sex should be discussed.
HARRY. Concentrating on the findings about social deviants.
MAN #2. *(Uneasy.)* Good for you.
HARRY. Great. So we can count you in to attend.
MAN #2. I sincerely wish you luck.
HARRY. I need it. *(Lights flash up on: Rudi and Man #3, now playing a different man.)*
MAN #3. *(Damon Runyonesque character, amused.)* The problem, pal — I just don't believe in your "cause."
RUDI. Then I've wasted *your* time. And mine.
MAN #3. However, if you'd like to go behind the dunes for a couple of minutes and … discuss it some more …
RUDI. *(Acting amused.)* You don't believe in my cause, but you will sneak behind … Don't you find that …
MAN #3. … What? … *(A pissed-off Rudi doesn't answer.)* Don't I

find it — what?
RUDI. Sad. *(Lights up on Harry talking to Man #2.)*
MAN #2. *(Now playing a sweet, kindly man, opening his heart.)* Oh my. That is quite the brave thing you're doing. I congratulate you.
HARRY. So you'll attend?
MAN #2. *(Gentle.)* I wish I could, but … I'm just not that strong. I hope you understand.
HARRY. … Go to hell! *(Harry grabs paper from the stunned man. Lights up on Rudi and Man #3.)*
MAN # 3. *(Now slightly fey.)* And over there is the Marion Davies estate.
RUDI. Yes, so I've been told —
MAN #3. My fiancée would never let me go to a meeting like that. It would give her the wrong idea.
RUDI. *(Incredulous.)* Your fiancée?! *(Tempering his rage at the man's hypocrisy.)* … Congratulations. On your upcoming — nuptials. *(Lights up on a growingly frustrated Harry now with Man #2.)*
MAN #2. *(Now very refined, whispering.)* That kind of meeting, I couldn't possibly —
HARRY. Just get away from me! *(As Harry stalks off, lights up on Rudi and Man #3, this time with a Texas accent.)*
MAN #3. *(Not the brightest.)* My father would kill me. I mean, wouldn't yours?
RUDI. He committed suicide when I was eight.
MAN #3. *(Not remotely perturbed.)* … Then the rest of your family.
RUDI. Most of them — except for my aunt and mother — died in Auschwitz.
MAN # 3. *(Doesn't have a clue what that is.)* Auschwitz? That sounds familiar.
RUDI. … It's a concentration camp. They were killed for who they were. Don't think it couldn't happen here.
MAN #3. Oh come on. I very much doubt that.
RUDI. Ah. Exactly what we presumed in Austria. First a government uses fear to keep people under their thumbs — *(Lights up on Harry talking to another man as Rudi continues talking to first.)*
HARRY. *(Finishing Rudi's thought.)* — Blaming everything on the enemy.
RUDI. Or a scapegoat. But who could that be?
HARRY. The blacks. No. They're already beginning to organize — gain strength.

RUDI. And the Holocaust is too recent to put the Jews in that position. So the natural scapegoat —
HARRY. The *one* group of disenfranchised people who don't even know they're a group!
RUDI. Because they'd never been formed as a group.
HARRY. So action needs to be taken.
RUDI. *(Overlapping.)* So action needs to be taken.
HARRY. And quickly.
MAN #3 *(Weirdly amused.)* Well, not with me.
MAN #2. No thank you.
RUDI and HARRY. ... Fuck you! *(Both look to each other, frustrated. Yet amused they're experiencing the same rage. Blackout. Rudi exits. Lights up on a sign that reads "Music — Barometer of the Class Struggle." We're in a classroom with Harry. A student in his class enters [played by Man #1] tuning up his ukulele.)*
HARRY. And now, class, something a little less serious. Today in "Music: Our Weapon in the Class Struggle" — we leap back to the Middle Ages. To The Feast of Fools. To a song performed by yours truly and your fellow commie pal, Bob. *(Bob doesn't come out.)* It's okay. Don't be embarrassed. *(Bob Hull, [Man #2], an ebullient, effeminate man, enters wearing a blousy blonde woman's wig and acting like a scullery maid. Harry, acting aristocratic, cues Man #1, who strums opening chord.)*
HARRY/ARISTOCRAT. *(Whispering to audience, confessing.)*
ALAS, I'M QUITE CERTAIN THAT LOVE IS TRULY BLIND
BOB/WENCH. *(A dumb blonde/Judy Holliday accent.)*
HE IS KINGLY — BORN OF NOBLE BIRTH
HARRY/ARISTOCRAT.
BUT MY LOINS ACHE FOR SOMETHING OF ... THE EARTH
BOB/WENCH.
HIS HEART POUNDS FOR A —
(Whispers, like it's a forbidden word, as he pulls out a giant turnip with a smiling face. He uses another voice now, his "turnip" voice.)
TURNIP, hee-haw.
HARRY/ARISTOCRAT. *(Lovingly sings to the turnip.)*
OH, IT'S DIRTY AND IT'S COARSE
BOB/WENCH. *(Holding up turnip.)*
IF YOU BITE ME, I'M BITTER

(Spoken, to audience as the turnip.) And he likes bitter.
HARRY/ARISTOCRAT.
AND QUITE THE GOOD KIDDER
WHEN — SCRUBBED UP IT GLISTENS
BOB/WENCH. *(As turnip.)*
YOU'RE CRANKY-POO — I LISTEN
HARRY/ARISTOCRAT.
IS SHE HIGHBROW?
BOB/WENCH. *(As turnip, proudly.)*
NO I AIN'T!
HARRY/ARISTOCRAT.
THAT'S MY —
BOB/WENCH. *(As turnip.)*
THAT'S YOUR —
BOTH.
TURNIP
(Harry sweetly leans in and kisses … the turnip.)
OUR LOVE IS PERFECTION
HARRY/ARISTOCRAT.
AND WILL RUIN MY LIFE
BOB/WENCH. *(As turnip.)* … Huh?!
HARRY/ARISTOCRAT.
OH THE BEST UPPER CLASSES
NEVER RUB WITH THE MASSES
A TURNIP CANNOT BE A WIFE
BOB/WENCH. *(As turnip, hurt.)* Why not?
HARRY/ARISTOCRAT. People will talk. And throw stones. *(Accusing.)* If you *just* hadn't been a turnip. *(Wench turns turnip. On the other side is a sad face.)*
I NEED —
BOB/WENCH.
HE NEEDS
BOTH.
A WIFE! *(End song.)*
HARRY. Thank you, Bob, for joining me in recreating The Feast of Fools — which was performed in medieval days by the Société Mattachine — an all-male organization. They encouraged cross-dressing, singing bawdy songs, and drinking to excess!
BOB. Hee-haw! Come on, hee-haw, Harry.
HARRY. … But even more importantly, they parodied the follies

of kings and church. And got so popular that they spread throughout Europe —

BOB. *(Jumping in, OVERLY enthusiastic.)* Called *Matassins* in France, *Mattacino* in Italy, *Mattachino* in Spain!

HARRY. *(Explaining Bob's knowledge.)* This is the third time Bob's taken this class! … The Mattachine troupes were not only funny on the outside, but deep down had a vital political message. They were multi-layered like — *(Realizing, thinking of Rudi.)* like a cameo … Next week, Negro spirituals — which were often used as a secret language. For instance, a lot of songs were about the Underground Railroad. Including: *(Singing, getting emotional.)*

SWING LOW, SWEET CHARIOT
COMING FOR TO CARRY ME — HOME

Which was actually code. Letting people know they were going to break away that night and head up north. *(Sings, tearing up.)*

SWING LOW — SWEET CHARIOT
COMING FOR TO CARRY ME —

(Spoken, crying.) Sorry about "the sprinkler." Something about music and politics, just gets me all weepy.

BOB. And why not?! It's amazing. There they were — singing out — communicating ideas and plans right under the noses of the authorities without them ever suspecting. It's beautiful.

HARRY. … That's it for today. Next week, we'll also be discussing "The Christmas Carol — as Guerilla Warfare." Good night and keep fighting the good fight! *(To Bob.)* As always, thanks for helping out, Bob.

BOB. *(Exuberant.)* Making an ass out of myself! What more could anyone want to do in life? *(Tinge of melancholy.)* It's actually the most fun I've had all week. *(Meanwhile, Harry goes and takes the manifesto from his bag.)*

HARRY. Before you go, you need to see —

BOB. Oh, that thing about North Korea. I signed it.

HARRY. No. This is different. And except for my Rudi, *(Correcting himself.)* uh, Rudi, no one's really shown a hell of a lot of interest in it. *(Harry holds it out. Bob takes it.)*

BOB. *(Overly cheery.)* I'll look it over. Bye. Hee-haw. Hee-haw! *(As Bob heads out, Harry stands there alone. Hopeful. Lights fade down on him and then shift as Rudi enters. Harry and Rudi stand together. It's a very windy November 11, 1950.)*

RUDI. *(Uneasy.)* I thought you told him three-thirty. It's past four.

HARRY. He picked the time, not me.
RUDI. Something feels wrong. What exactly did he say about the document?
HARRY. He definitely wants to talk to me about it.
RUDI. Do you think this is a trap?
HARRY. Fifteen minutes ago I did. Now …
RUDI. Yes?
HARRY. I'm certain.
RUDI. Let's go.
HARRY. I can't. I gave my word I'd be here. But you go. *(Rudi remains. As they continue waiting, Chuck [Man #1], wearing glasses, rushes in from behind and awkwardly wraps his arms around Harry. Chuck is smart, oddly precise, thoughtful. With perhaps a slight Minnesotan accent. As Harry breaks away, Chuck falls to the ground.)*
RUDI. *(Firmly.) Was wollen sie?!* [What do you want?]
CHUCK. Aren't you — *(Bob races onstage, singing the gospel song "His Eye is on the Sparrow," holding up the manifesto.)*
BOB. *(Sings.)*
I SING BECAUSE I'M HAPPY —
(Spoken.) Harry, I could have written this myself — *(Suddenly seeing Chuck on the ground.)* What happened to you?
CHUCK. *(Not wanting to ruin this meeting.)* … I tripped … That's all … That's all. *(Now Rudi and Harry know everything's fine — that Chuck is with them.)*
BOB. *(Suddenly very concerned.)* Are you all right?
CHUCK. My glasses just fell off. I'm normally more coordinated. I'm fine.
BOB. I'm helping you up anyway. *(And he does. Then Bob turns to Harry.)* This is Chuck. My friend. Oh hell, we live together.
CHUCK. *(A man of few words, but doesn't beat around the bush.)* Since 1940. Minnesota.
BOB. Although no longer really together. Just living-wise. We see other people on the side —
CHUCK. *(Not happy with the situation, more private.)* You don't need to explain everything to them.
HARRY. And this is Rudi.
RUDI. *(Slyly.)* We don't live together, but for about six months we've been in … cahoots.
BOB. So I guess that makes you cahooters! Although maybe not — since you don't have a cahooter between ya. *(Chuck laughs. He*

loves Bob's ridiculous sense of humor.)
RUDI. Let's talk someplace more private.
HARRY. The top of the hill — overlooking Silver Lake. *(The lights shift and the group has a conversation unheard by the audience. Finally they make it to the top of the hill and look out. When we finally hear them speak, they don't look at each other at first, but just look out at the view. Each one having his own memory. Slowly, however, they look at each other more and more, connecting.)*
BOB. *(Telling his story.)* And I just couldn't stop staring at my next door neighbor's son, mowing the lawn —
RUDI. *(Telling his story.)* With his shirt off —
CHUCK. *(Telling his story.)* My mother said, "Stop staring."
HARRY. *(Telling his story.)* So I stopped —
RUDI. At least so openly. I learned —
CHUCK. The quick glance.
HARRY. The fast look away.
BOB. Unless I was on a bus and then I'd stare —
RUDI. Without shame.
HARRY. I became a master at making excuses —
BOB. Bending the truth —
RUDI. Outright lying!
CHUCK. "I'm a people watcher."
BOB. "Oh, I just like looking!"
RUDI. My aunt would say, *"Der Mann ist so attraktiv."*
HARRY. "I guess."
CHUCK. "I can't really tell if a man is attractive." *(All stare at a man passing by whom they find extremely good-looking. As he finally disappears out of view, one or two even sigh. Then they look around to see if anyone else caught them looking.)*
BOB. And as each day passed
HARRY. I got better
RUDI. And better
CHUCK. At concealing
RUDI. Evading
HARRY. Holding in
BOB. My feelings
RUDI. Because my family
CHUCK. Friends
BOB. Would be —
CHUCK. — horrified.

HARRY. Beat the crap out of me.
RUDI. So disappointed.
CHUCK. And I held in my emotions because, well,
BOB. I was ashamed.
CHUCK. *(Surprised.)* ... You, too?
BOB. That's hard to believe?
RUDI. Well yes. You are *so* out there.
HARRY. I can't believe —
BOB. *(To Rudi.)* Really?
HARRY. — That you never told Chuck.
CHUCK. *(Realizing.)* Huh.
BOB. It never came up.
HARRY. After all these years?
RUDI. Well Harry, it's not as if you ...
HARRY. What?
RUDI. Really open up. And talk.
HARRY. Well it's not as if you ask me about myself! How'm I supposed to know you're interested in something if you don't ask me!?
RUDI. Oh please, I ask —
HARRY. And you know, you don't exactly open up either, *mein* ... *(Searching for word.) Schnitzel!* You do not open up either! *(Beat.)*
RUDI. *Mein Schnitzel? (Harry shrugs. It was an embarrassing word choice.)*
CHUCK. But for some reason, today we did.
BOB. Huh.
RUDI. Why? *(They look out again.)*
BOB. *(Glib.)* We were inspired — looking out at the lovely village of Silver Lake?
HARRY. No. *(Harry stretches out his arm and says sincerely.)* Home ... We're home.
RUDI. *(Placing his hand on top of Harry's.) Ja. Heimat. (Bob places his hand on top of Rudi's, then Chuck does as well.)*
CHUCK. *(Unsure.)* Home. *(They hold for a moment, then.)*
HARRY. Let history record, on this hill overlooking Silver Lake, the first four founding fathers of the Mattachine Society met — to discuss who we are — and to cry out — "No, we are not broken heterosexuals! No. We have our own unique consciousness much different from heterosexuals — "
RUDI. Because we see the world much differently —
BOB. Sing hallelujah!

HARRY. AND — that we are an oppressed minority. *(Bob and Chuck don't understand what he means.)*
BOB. *(Puzzled.)* … Explain.
HARRY. Every organization must have a theory.
CHUCK. As the Communist Party teaches us.
HARRY. *(Surprised, impressed.)* Correct.
BOB. *(Explaining.)* Back in Minneapolis, Chuck headed the *entire* Midwest Youth Division of the C.P. — *(Translating.)* Communist party.
CHUCK. They know what C.P. means.
HARRY. *(Getting back to his theory.)* So our theory: unlike the Jews who are an oppressed *religious* minority —
RUDI. And the Negroes, an oppressed *ethnic* minority —
HARRY. *We* are an oppressed *sexual* minority. How do we take ourselves out of the oppressed category? First, we have got to get a better grasp of who we are. Define ourselves.
RUDI. Then pass along that information. Hopefully, as the country better understands us AND we become more visible, society's views will change for the better.
CHUCK. *(Skeptical.)* So the more they see us, the more they might — *like* us?
BOB. Or at least tolerate us.
CHUCK. *(A new idea.)* AND — the more we get into the thick of society, the more political and financial power we *just* might acquire.
HARRY. Precisely. *(Impressed.)* We have got some very smart founding fathers.
CHUCK. *(Plucky.)* Yes, you do.
HARRY. … Let it also be proclaimed today that from now on, all major votes must be unanimous on whatever actions we take.
CHUCK. *(Respectfully.)* Excuse me, but before you state that every vote must be unanimous, I think we should vote on *that.*
HARRY. But I'm giving you the power.
CHUCK. *(Understanding the danger.)* And the responsibility with that power.
BOB. *(Realizing.)* Oh! So if something ever goes wrong, we'll all be to blame, not just Harry and Rudi.
CHUCK. That's right. *(To Harry.)* Which is why we ALL need to agree that's what we want.
RUDI. That makes perfect sense.
HARRY. But I'm giving you the damn power —

RUDI. Harry, you're not listening and you're bullying. *(Harry gets quiet. Sullen.)* So who thinks all major votes from now on must be unanimous with our core group, the four of us?
BOB. I do.
CHUCK. I agree.
RUDI. So do I … Harry?
HARRY. *I'm* the one who thought it up!
RUDI. Harry?
HARRY. Agreed. *(Warmly.)* Agreed. *(They stare out at Silver Lake for a moment.)*
BOB. It's a little scary what we're doing.
HARRY. *(Checking watch.)* Damn. I can't be late for dinner again. My wife would kill me. Gotta go. *(Harry exits. Bob and Chuck stand there, stunned.)*
BOB. He's kidding, right?
RUDI. He's been married eleven years.
CHUCK. Any children?
RUDI. I think two.
BOB. And his wife's name?
RUDI. I never asked.
CHUCK. So Harry was right. You *don't* ask him about things. *(And as Rudi takes that in and Bob and Chuck exit, lights shift to … Nigel Butler [Man #3] entering, examining Rudi's sketchbook. Rudi stands there as he does.)*
NIGEL. *(Thick British accent, a wicked grin.)* And to make the houndstooth check that immense, well — it's damn cheeky. In a good way. Which is why …
RUDI. Yes?
NIGEL. I might groom you. To be one of my designers.
RUDI. *(Thrilled.)* Mr. Butler —
NIGEL. Nigel.
RUDI. Nigel, I'm stunned by your offer.
NIGEL. I said — "might" — groom you. Next meeting, I'll take you out to lunch. Bring in some more sketches. AND, bring in your wife.
RUDI. I'm not married.
NIGEL. Then your girlfriend.
RUDI. I don't have one.
NIGEL. Then you're single? *(Rudi is silent, not answering that.)* If I'm grooming someone to be a top designer, they'll need to be out in the spotlight. What they do reflects on the entire company.

RUDI. *(Acting innocent.)* What are you telling me?
NIGEL. Come off it. You don't play naïve well … You really think *my* name is Nigel Butler? *(Dropping British accent and his "mask," confiding.)* Mark Pincus. Born on the Grand Concourse. Picked up my dulcet tones listening to Leslie Howard in *Gone with the Wind.* Another Jew … You're lucky. You've already got that snooty European thing going. 'Course, now I've got it. AND, a wife and two kids. *(Picking up the British accent again, slyly.)* Catch up to me, old chum. Or at least …
RUDI. Yes?
NIGEL. Don't make it so obvious. *(A stunned Rudi doesn't know what to say. Nigel exits. Rudi stands there, agitated, as lights shift and we're in Bob and Chuck's rec room. Harry enters and begins to set up a few chairs. Rudi does as well. He's still very unsettled.)*
HARRY. I don't like it. It makes me uneasy. Violates one of my bylaws.
RUDI. But Bob and Chuck volunteered their rec room —
HARRY. That's not the point! I don't like using the same meeting place twice.
RUDI. We haven't been here in almost a year.
HARRY. Remember to hide the phone.
RUDI. I know! *(They continue setting up chairs.)* Harry?
HARRY. Yes, Rudi.
RUDI. What's it all leading to?
HARRY. Leading to? The Mattachine Society is gathering numbers.
RUDI. A few one week, then we lose a few the next.
HARRY. Well, without something to unite us —
RUDI. — We're treading water. Although when I asked what this is leading to, I meant us.
HARRY. Oh … Why are you bringing this up now?
RUDI. *(Not answering.)* Are you becoming strong enough to leave your wife? If not, we should end this — before we get in too deep. *(Beat. Harry's thrown.)*
HARRY. *(Accusatory, changing subject.)* If you had just gotten us Vincente Minnelli. Or any of those Hollywood, high-profile —
RUDI. Christopher Isherwood promised to give some money.
HARRY. *(Surprised.)* … Really? And let us use his name? *(Rudi is silent. Obviously not.)* Then it's worthless. *He's* completely worthless. *(Beat, half-heartedly.)* Although his money *is* good. How many new ones today?

RUDI. Just one. His name is Dale. Apparently he works at a carnival. *(In another part of the stage, Dale [Man #3] a headstrong, blue collar guy enters and stands on a street corner, waiting.)*
HARRY. A carny guy! And he's temperamental?
RUDI. Maybe he's rough trade.
HARRY. How do you even know that expression?
RUDI. Oh, Harry.
HARRY. ... How do we know he's one of us? *(Annoyed.)* A carny guy.
RUDI. You're not exactly a typical temperamental yourself.
HARRY. Should I be offended by that remark or pleased?
RUDI. Your choice.
HARRY. I'm offended! ... *And* pleased ... What the hell is that about?
RUDI. I couldn't say. *(On that street corner, Bob approaches Dale.)*
BOB. *(Secretive, softly.)* Dale.
DALE. *(Loud.)* Bob!
BOB. *(Softly.)* Follow me.
DALE. Hold on! Where we going?
BOB. *(Softly.)* To the meeting.
DALE. Where the hell is it?
BOB. I can't give out that information. In case you're an informant.
DALE. We've been dating six months.
BOB. These are Harry's rules.
DALE. You listen to everything this guy says?
BOB. *(Dryly.)* Same way I listen to everything *you* say. *(Meanwhile Harry and Rudi continue arranging the chairs in the rec room.)*
RUDI. *(Getting back to his point.)* It's just that — the more we work together ... the closer we get.
HARRY. I agree.
RUDI. And the more difficult your other life becomes. For me. *(Harry keeps rearranging chairs, not wanting to deal with this. While back outside ...)*
BOB. *(Talking softer.)* We're almost there.
DALE. Hold on. Don't you live in this neighborhood?
BOB. Right here.
DALE. So I'm finally meeting Chuck.
BOB. He won't be attending this meeting. *(Rudi, angered, finally blurts out.)*
RUDI. I am never even part of your holidays. How do you think that makes me feel? *(And as Harry really takes that in.)*

DALE. *(To Bob, puzzled.)* Am I ever gonna meet Chuck?
BOB. I don't like my paramours mixing.
DALE. How come?
BOB. Some things are better kept separate. Like communism and Christianity, bourbon and barbiturates. Negroes and non-Negroes.
DALE. You kidding?
BOB. *(Ignoring that.)* This way. *(Bob exits, followed by Dale.)*
HARRY. *(To Rudi, deciding to do this.)* Come to our Christmas party.
RUDI. *(Stunned.)* Uh … Yours and Anita's?
HARRY. I know it's not much. *(Rudi doesn't respond.)* Is it?
RUDI. *(Sees Harry trying.)* At least we'll be together.
HARRY. Remember to bring a present.
RUDI. *(Re: invitation being a good idea.)* You're certain?
HARRY. *(Trying to be lighthearted.)* Definitely. Because without a present, you would NOT be welcome. *(Rudi laughs. Harry goes to Rudi, sweetly kisses him.)* Is that more romantic? *(Rudi firmly/quietly takes control, kisses Harry, begins to remove his shirt.)* We have guests arriving any — Rudi! *(The phone begins to ring.)* We should get that … It could be important — *(Rudi pushes Harry down.)* I thought *I* was the aggressor in this relationship.
RUDI. That was yesterday. *(Suddenly Bob races in, in a panic, followed by Dale.)*
BOB. You haven't covered it yet?! *(Bob runs to the phone and hides it. Meanwhile, Rudi jumps off of Harry who quickly puts his shirt back on.)* You were supposed to cover it right away!
DALE. *(Seeing Harry half-naked.)* What's going on?
RUDI. *(Changing the subject.)* Bob — uh — read that telephones could be used to bug a room.
DALE. No, I meant what's going on with the two of / you —
HARRY. *(Interrupting on /.)* So we always put the phone in a drawer.
BOB. And put a pillow over it. Right away.
RUDI. I'm sorry, Bob.
BOB. This is my place. I'm the one who'd get arrested!
RUDI. Honestly, we are sorry.
DALE. I think the police got more interesting people to hunt down than Bob and Chuck.
HARRY. *(Confrontational.)* You'd be surprised.
DALE. *(Confrontational back.)* Yeah, I would be. 'Cuz before I worked at a carnival, I was a cop. *(Harry and Rudi look at each other.)*

BOB. That's right — eat your heart out, guys. I'm dating a cop.
HARRY. You sure you're not still a cop?
DALE. Why, do ya want me to frisk you? *(Harry doesn't laugh.)*
BOB. Harry, Rudi, this is Dale.
DALE. Although you can call me Dale … *(Deciding to one-up Harry and bravely say his last name.)* Dale — *Jennings.*
HARRY. Dale — Jennings?
DALE. That's right. *(To Harry.)* And your name again?
HARRY. Harry … *(Deciding whether he'll risk saying his last name.)* Hay!
DALE. Hello Harry Hay. *(To Rudi.)* Dale Jennings. And you? *(Beat. Rudi considers, then.)*
RUDI. Rudi.
DALE. Rudi what?
RUDI. … Rudi. *(Harry looks for Rudi to say his last name. Rudi has no intention of doing that. Harry's stunned. Blackout. An F major chord is heard. We hear voices raised in song and a ukulele playing as lights up on Harry and Anita's Christmas party. Rudi and Harry, wearing a silly hat, and all of Harry's communist friends belt out the final verse of "The Twelve Days of Christmas.")*
VOICES. *(With a flourish.)*

FOUR CALLING BIRDS, THREE FRENCH HENS, TWO TURTLE DOVES
AND A PARTRIDGE — IN — A — PEAR — TREE!

(All applaud. Man # 2 and Man #3 exit.)
UKULELE STUDENT. *(From communist meeting.)* Classical! Something classical — and religious.
HARRY. Anita knows a million of them.
UKULELE STUDENT. Please, your wife has had enough solos today! Harry, you sing.
HARRY. *(Loves to sing.)* Me? … No … I'm not really a singer —
UKULELE STUDENT. Okay, then maybe Susan has a song she'd like —
HARRY. *(Dying to sing.)* "Sleepers, Wake," I could sing that!
RUDI. *(On the other side of the room.)* I know that one as well.
HARRY. You do?
RUDI. Well, if you're referring to *"Wachet auf."*
HARRY. Yes. You know it? I mean you're, well —
RUDI. *(Interrupting.)* What?
HARRY. *(Whispering, mischievously.)* Jewish.

RUDI. And Austrian.
HARRY. Well then — Rudi?
RUDI. Yes, Harry?
HARRY. Let's sing it together.
RUDI. *(Surprised and touched at the offer.)* Really? In the original German?
HARRY. In the original *English. I'll* start. *(Ukulele Student plays. As Harry and Rudi sing we see the love that exists between them. Sometimes their hands get too close, almost touching. They pull away for fear of being caught. Throughout the song, Harry and Rudi realize that these lyrics have a double meaning.)*

"SLEEPERS, WAKE!" A VOICE COMMANDS US

RUDI.

AND HEED THE WORDS THAT HEAVEN HANDS US

HARRY and RUDI. *(Re: Rudi pushing Harry to awaken, embrace being a couple.)*

"AWAKE, JERUSALEM, AWAKE!"

HARRY.

MIDNIGHT'S PEACE HAS NOW BEEN BROKEN

RUDI.

BY URGENT SUMMONS CLEARLY SPOKEN

HARRY and RUDI.

AND THUS IT'S TIME OUR PART TO TAKE

(As Rudi and Harry continue softly singing at Harry's Christmas party, Ukulele Student exits. Lights shift down on them and up on a street corner. Dale and Bob enter in the middle of a conversation. We don't hear their words, but it's obvious Bob is dumping Dale as a boyfriend. Returning a ring that Dale gave him. Bob exits. Dale stands there — upset, not knowing what to do with his emotions. Harry and Rudi continue singing, still half in darkness.)

COME FORTH, YE VIRGINS WISE:
THE BRIDEGROOM COMES, ARISE!
ALLELUIA!
EACH LAMP BE BRIGHT WITH READY LIGHT
TO GRACE THE MARRIAGE FEAST TONIGHT.

(Dale goes to a men's room. Pees. Another man [Man #1] also stands by the urinal. Stares at Dale. The man reaches for Dale's crotch. Dale immediately jumps back — looks at it him as if to say "I'm not interested" and heads out. However, the man heads out after him as the singing in the other scene continues throughout. Harry and Rudi con-

tinue singing, still half in darkness.)

ZION HEARS THE WATCHMEN SINGING
HER HEART WITH JOYFUL HOPE IS SPRINGING
SHE WAKES AND HURRIES THROUGH THE NIGHT
FORTH HE COMES, HER BRIDEGROOM GLORIOUS
IN STRENGTH OF GRACE, IN TRUTH VICTORIOUS
THOUGH LONG DELAYED, HE'S NOW IN SIGHT
ALL HAIL! GOD'S GLORIOUS SON
ALL HAIL OH HOLY ONE.

(Dale heads out followed by the other man, who suddenly blocks his path, shows his badge, then violently handcuffs Dale. As Dale is shoved offstage, crying out in pain, the song continues and lights up on Harry's party.)

ALLELUIA! THE JOYFUL CALL WE ANSWER ALL

(Phone rings. Harry stops singing and goes to answer it.)

RUDI.

AND FOLLOW TO THE BRIDAL HALL.
LAMB OF GOD, THE HEAVENS ADORE YOU
LET SAINTS AND ANGELS —

(Rudi stops singing as he sees Harry on the phone, clearly hearing bad news. Lights shift to the Chuckwagon Diner with Harry, Rudi, Bob, Chuck, and a bruised-up Dale. As before, they try to keep their voices down. However, they begin to get louder as the scene goes on without them even being aware of it.)

DALE. Don't worry. I'll pay each of you back in full.

RUDI. We're not worried.

BOB. *(Annoyed.)* Please, the fifty bucks to get you out of jail is the *least* of your troubles.

DALE. You really need to be that catty? Especially right now? *(Nursing a wound.)* Ow.

BOB. Well if you hadn't been so stupid.

DALE. I did nothing wrong! Sure, I was feeling rotten 'cuz you dumped me. Was *thinking* 'bout doing something stupid. But didn't.

BOB. *(Interrupting.)* I didn't dump you. I just thought it was getting too serious.

DALE. *(To Harry.)* Tell someone you like them — suddenly they think you're serious.

HARRY. Because you *are* serious about him! Don't be ashamed of that. It's not your fault that Bob is a lightweight when it comes to dealing with deeper feelings.

BOB. Does someone not see me *right* here in the Chuckwagon?!

CHUCK. *(Hating to say it out loud, but …)* You *are* a lightweight.
RUDI. *(Slyly.)* And if Harry can see it, it must be incredibly obvious.
CHUCK. Until you know who you really are, Bob, you can never be in a relationship. At least not a real one.
BOB. Why are we all picking on sweet, funny Bob?! I wasn't the one who just got arrested in a men's room! … Besides, *I* know who I am! Look at me. I'm a helluva lot more out there than the rest of you!
RUDI. Or is that your façade? Hiding something deeper and darker underneath.
BOB. *("Acting" surprised.)* … Oh! You're talking to *me?* I thought you were talking about yourself.
CHUCK. *(To Dale, with some quiet bitterness.)* I should have warned you earlier: none of Bob's boyfriends ever last.
DALE. So it's not me. Or you. It's —
CHUCK. — Bob … It's Bob!
BOB. *This* — is why I disapprove of my exes hanging around each other. *(Seeing Dale still in pain. Not easy for Bob to talk about feelings.)* So one of the uh — inmates … Is that how you got those bruises?
DALE. *(Shakes his head "no.")* One of the cops … It looks horrible, doesn't it? *(All disagree — "Not at all" "No!" … etc.)*
BOB. It's very butch. *(Pause. The room grows serious.)*
RUDI. *(To Harry.)* So Harry?
HARRY. Hmm?
RUDI. What does Dale do now?
DALE. *(Worried.)* Yeah.
HARRY. *(To Dale.)* Plead guilty to what they call "vag-lewd." Vagrancy and lewdness. Then the court will make you pay from three hundred dollars — to three thousand —
DALE. Three thousand?
HARRY. The more you pay, the less jail time.
DALE. *(Freaking out, trying to hide it.)* I don't have three C-notes, much less three thousand. *(Firmly.)* Gimme another choice.
HARRY. There *is* none. *(Anxious beat.)*
RUDI. Think some more, Harry.
DALE. Yeah. Think.
HARRY. Everyone's always pleaded guilty. 'Cuz if you don't — it goes to court. And then it's printed in the papers for everyone to see that Dale Jennings is a homosexual.
RUDI. Voice down. No need to ruin his reputation before our legal system gets their chance.

DALE. I'm a carnival roustabout. What kind of reputation do I even have?
CHUCK. Dale — you're not living on an island. If the carnival — uh — people — find out, they will definitely look at you differently.
DALE. You mean all the *other* freaks will judge me?
CHUCK. Any time you try to get credit — or a job — buy a house — it'll be on your public record.
RUDI. People may act charming to your face, but who knows what they're really thinking.
DALE. I'm a thirty-five-year-old "single" man. They're thinking something already.
HARRY. *(Getting an idea.)* ... Well then ...
DALE. Yeah?
HARRY. Plead that you're innocent of all charges.
DALE. You think a jury will believe it?
HARRY. *(Mulling it over.)* If you also admit — that you're a homosexual.
DALE. *(Incredulous.)* And the reason I'd —
CHUCK. *(Interrupting.)* Why would he want to do that?
HARRY. Because it's the truth ... Don't you see? Dale's only way of winning is to tell the truth. And that begins by admitting that he's temperamental. A LOT temperamental.
RUDI. A huge thing to confess.
HARRY. And earning him big points with the jury — for being so honest.
BOB. *(Catching on.)* I get it. So Dale admits that — yes he is a homosexual. *(Acting like a trial lawyer.)* "But no — members of the jury — he did NOT commit any acts of lewdness. So why is he in court right now? Because this cop — right there — set him up!"
CHUCK. Who is going to believe a cop would lie?
RUDI. Everyone. It's Los Angeles.
HARRY. And the beauty of it *is* — all of it's true!
RUDI. *(Realizing, half to himself.)* This is also the perfect moment for the Mattachine Society to press the issue that we're an oppressed minority. Because Dale is being accused of something he didn't do — just because of who he is.
HARRY. Exactly, Rudi. Exactly! *(Harry grabs Rudi and impulsively kisses him on the lips. Rudi pushes him away. Everyone else quickly looks around, nervous.)*
RUDI. What are you — ?!

HARRY. *(Stunned as well.)* Sorry. I forgot for a second that we're not just part of the air.
RUDI. *(Confused.)* Yet.
DALE. *(Uneasy.)* I need time to really think this through —
BOB. We'll ALL be right by your side. Right, guys?
RUDI. *(Torn.)* Of course.
HARRY. The entire time.
CHUCK. How will your wife react to that?
HARRY. Time to find out.
BOB. So we're on!
DALE. Wait, wait! *I* — haven't agreed to anything — !
BOB. *(His eyes ablaze.)* Dale. Baby! You gotta do it! Harry is right! Rudi is right! Even Chuck is right — though he's barely said a positive word. This is the moment we've all been waiting for. We thought we needed a famous leader to rally the troops. But no we don't!
HARRY. *(Jumping in — agreeing.)* Instead we need a cause.
RUDI. A beleaguered comrade we can fight for.
BOB. And Dale, baby, you're it!
HARRY. You're going to be our — Joan of Arc!
BOB. *(Working himself into a frenzy.)* Yes, our — our Marian Anderson! Our — uh —
CHUCK. *(Still unsure of their plan — and oddly perturbed there's not a historical male equivalent.)* There must be at least *one* male example.
BOB. Who cares if they've all been ladies so far! You're gonna change that, Dale … Sort of. You gotta do it! You gotta! *(Pointing with his finger.)* The Hinger of Fistory points — *(The others laugh.)* I mean the Finger of History —
HARRY. No. You were right the first time. *(To Dale.)* Dale. The Hinger of Fistory points … to you. With the other four musketeers right next to you! *(Harry puts out his hand. Bob puts his on top of Harry's. Then an anxious Chuck finally jumps into the mix and places his hand. Harry looks over, curious that Rudi hasn't put his hand in yet. Finally Rudi does. They all look to Dale. To see what he'll do. He considers. The guys look at each other concerned that he won't do it.)*
RUDI. … Whatever you decide, we will understand. *(Dale looks at each of the men. And then make his decision. Dale places his hand firmly on top of theirs. He's in. Blackout.)*

End of Act One

ACT TWO

At rise: Harry's asleep. Dreaming.

HARRY. ... Hurry ... Wait! ... wait. *(Suddenly remembering, concerned.)* ... George. *(Harry drifts back into sleep. Four women quietly enter one by one. Played by our four other actors.)*
WOMAN #1. *(Played by Man #2. A quiet sob.)* Uhh.
WOMAN #2. *(Played by Man #1. Perky.)* I'll serve tea?
WOMAN #3. *(Played by Man #3. Suspicious.)* This discussion group. There's something more behind it, isn't there?!
WOMAN #4. *(Played by Rudi. Angry.)* Character weakness!
WOMAN #1. *(A quiet sob.)* Uhh.
WOMAN #2. I'll serve tea?
WOMAN #3. This discussion group. There's something more behind it, isn't there?
WOMAN #4. Character weakness! *(An anxious Harry looks at all four and then decides to go to Woman #1.)*
HARRY. *(To Woman #1, softly, tenderly.)* I knew it would be toughest to tell you.
WOMAN #1. *(A sob.)* Uhh.
HARRY. *(Very personal, as if talking to a lover.)* I wish I could but I just can't stay. You know how much I'm in love with ... the Communist Party. But being a homosexual and involved with the Mattachine Society would be a security risk to the Party.
WOMAN #1. *(Still sobbing.)* But you're such — such an original thinker. AND — a hard worker!
HARRY. That's high praise coming from the district section organizer.
WOMAN #1. *(Pulling herself together.)* So Harry.
HARRY. Yes, Miriam.
WOMAN #1. Are there other ... AC/DCs in the party?
HARRY. Like the Communist Party, we never reveal the identity of another without his permission.
WOMAN #1. I never thought of homosexuality as a political

issue. YOU have a code as well?
HARRY. *(Half to himself.)* Who we are.
WOMAN #2. *(Perky.)* I'll serve tea?
HARRY. *(To Woman #2.)* Terrific. Now that we're going ahead with this case, we're also going to need an address in order to legally register the Society. I can't exactly do it at my place —
WOMAN #2. *(Finishing his sentence.)* — then we'll use mine!
HARRY. Beautiful. Would you — uh — also mind being Treasurer?
WOMAN #2. Mind? And I'll open a special account at my bank — for the Society dues.
HARRY. *(Pleased, but concerned.)* Really? … This could "earn" you an FBI file. You do realize —
WOMAN #2. *(Interrupting.)* Yes I do … *(A little nervous and yet.)* Things must be done properly.
HARRY. … Which is also why at every discussion group or board meeting everyone either wears a suit or a jacket and tie.
WOMAN #2. Very smart of you. That's also why I'm serving tea. Things must be done properly.
HARRY. You're amazing, Mother.
WOMAN #2. *(As Harry's mother.)* No, my son is. And I like serving tea.
HARRY. *(As a little boy.)* And *I* like your hat.
WOMAN #2. *(Trying to hide that she's not pleased.)* Of course you do … But that little piece of news? Keep it under YOUR hat.
HARRY. *(As a precocious little boy.)* Please, Mother! I'm only nine, but I know that.
WOMAN #2. Already? How?
HARRY. *(To himself.)* Who we are.
WOMAN #3. *(Tough, ominous.)* This discussion group. There's something more behind it, isn't there?
HARRY. *(Guarded, an adult again.)* What do you mean?
WOMAN #3. There's an organization behind it. Isn't there?
HARRY. Well — uh — we had to organize to arrange the meeting place, come up with the topic "Should Homosexuals Marry?"
WOMAN #3. Which is ridiculous! To have masculine homosexuals marry women and then just have their affairs on the side — that does NOT take into account the suffering of the woman. So I definitely do NOT believe in homosexuals marrying.
HARRY. Agreed. Although I understand the man's dilemma.
WOMAN #3. Of course. Because you're masculine.

HARRY. I can't help that.
WOMAN #3. Why should you? I'm a masculine woman and don't care. Although I would never marry. Unless it were to another woman. *(For a moment, they seriously consider that possibility, but then laugh. It's ludicrous that could ever happen.)* So I want to join the board of your society.
HARRY. My society?
WOMAN #3. I can tell you're the leader. *(Harry is silent.)* Would I be the first woman on the board?
HARRY. Yes.
WOMAN #3. Good. I like that. I'm Ruth Bernhard.
HARRY. Harry Hay.
WOMAN #3. *(As Ruth.)* Good to meet you, Harry Hay. My "heterosexual" homosexual friend. *(Harry takes that in, not completely pleased.)*
HARRY. *(To himself.)* Who we are.
WOMAN #4. *(Rage.)* Character weakness!
HARRY. If that's how you feel, Anita —
WOMAN #2. *(Concerned.)* You told Anita?
HARRY. Last week.
WOMAN #4. *(As Anita.)* You need to go to a shrink and get this rooted out of you! … Rooted out of you!
HARRY. I don't care what the shrinks say, they're wrong. You can't root something out — when it's your roots. My roots.
WOMAN #4. It's just a physical addiction! A pure lustful, physical addiction! I guess I should be grateful you haven't acted on it yet. Thank you for at least being respectful of our marriage vows!
HARRY. … You're welcome.
WOMAN #4. But to be so public with this organization. I mean first you're a member of the Communist Party —
HARRY. Well so were you!
WOMAN #4. Well yes, but now this!
HARRY. Homosexuals are a scapegoated minority. As a Jew, you understand that situation —
WOMAN #4. But you're not even one of them yet. Why can't you let someone else do the organizing? You always have to be out in front … Who else is doing this with you?
HARRY. … One fellow escaped from the Nazis. The rest of his family — their homes, factories, all taken from them. He saw his uncle and grandmother forced by the Nazis to scrub the streets of

Vienna in the dead of winter. Then they were shipped off and killed.
WOMAN #4. *(Touched.)* Oh … well with him, you can see why he feels the need to speak up.
HARRY. *(Dawning on him.)* … And the need to succeed.
WOMAN #4. *(Realizing.)* You love this man, don't you? … Don't you?
HARRY. Yes.
WOMAN #4. You are so predictable. *(Off Harry's puzzlement.)* Going from one Jew to the next! Your girlfriend before me, wasn't she also Jewish?
HARRY. AND, political. Do you want me to move out?
WOMAN #4. You'll move out when I tell you to!
WOMAN #2. *(As Harry's mother.)* It's nice having people around the house again. They even drop by when you haven't scheduled a meeting.
HARRY. What?!
WOMAN #2. Don't worry. They're fine boys. Sometimes when one of their love affairs break up, they come and talk to me about it.
HARRY. Well I'll make sure they don't bother —
WOMAN #4. Failure. Shame and failure!
WOMAN #2. It's fine. I mostly listen.
HARRY. Just listen?
WOMAN #2. That's all they need.
WOMAN #4. Failure and shame! … Harry. *(Beat. Harry says nothing. He just listens to his wife.)*
HARRY. *(Honest.)* … I'm listening. … Really.
WOMAN #4. And shame … I am so ashamed.
HARRY. *(Surprised.) You're* ashamed?
WOMAN #4. Failing *you.* Our marriage.
HARRY. But you didn't — *(Pause.)* I'm listening.
WOMAN #4. Eleven years, I knew you were … *(Proudly.)* But still — *I* succeeded. Until … failure … And shame. *(Beat. Now that he's listening to her.)* But now it's time … for a divorce.
HARRY. Anita … thank you … Miriam — goodbye … Welcome, Ruth … You are amazing, Mother. And your hats.
WOMAN #2. But keep that under your —
HARRY. *(As if finishing her sentence.)* — who we are.
WOMAN #1. There's a code in the Mattachine Society?
HARRY. Who we are.
WOMAN #3. My heterosexual, homosexual —

HARRY. Who we are.
WOMAN #4. You love this man, don't you?
HARRY. Who we are. *(As these voices grow louder and louder saying "But keep that under your" "There's a code in the Mattachine Society?" "My homosexual, heterosexual" "You love this man, don't you?" — Harry keeps saying "who we are" until finally he screams — waking up.)* Who we — Ahhh! *(Lights blackout as all the "women" exit. Then lights swiftly up on Harry and Rudi in their bedroom.)*
RUDI. Are you all right? … Another nightmare?
HARRY. The strange thing is — while I'm in the middle of it, it definitely seems like a nightmare. But when I wake up and you're next to me, it's more like a dream come true.
RUDI. *(Dryly.)* You Americans are so sentimental underneath your bravura. Flip over. I am making you feel good. *(Harry turns over on his stomach. Rudi starts to massage him. Harry grunts and groans as he does.)* I've read that people hold specific anxieties and fears in different parts of their body. Recently, it's tighter right here. Something bothering you?
HARRY. No. *(Rudi rubs him harder.)* Ow! Not so rough.
RUDI. *(Dryly.)* Take it. Like a man.
HARRY. My father's favorite expression.
RUDI. Well, they say you fall in love with someone just like your mother or father.
HARRY. I've fallen in love?
RUDI. *(Continues massaging.)* I think that YOU — are more like my mother.
HARRY. That doesn't make any sense.
RUDI. Why?
HARRY. The nature of our relationship.
RUDI. Why must our relationship be so black and white? Mimic the heteros … When I was eleven, I woke up one morning — sick of the sameness of my life. So instead of taking my regular seat at the table, I sat down in my mother's chair. My uncle and aunt started choking on their *Roggenbrot* — waiting for the twister called *"Meine Mutter"* that was about to spin into the room. And spin she did. Arms waving. Head whirling. Screaming: "Get out of my seat." I remained quietly in her chair. With a secret in my pocket. I knew that my mother — was a tornado. Tornadoes thrive on instability. Destroy the unstable balance of hot and cold air, they stop functioning. So instead of arguing with my Mother, I simply refused to fight back. With

nothing to push against, she grew weaker. Till finally she just — stopped — *(Growing quieter.)* screaming. And let me eat my meal in peace. In her chair … Every few weeks I would change seats. Be my uncle. My aunt. Or even myself. Each time the twister *"Meine Mutter"* whipped into the room. Each time I put myself in the eye of the storm. And waited it out.

HARRY. Wish I could be that cool-headed.

RUDI. How are things going with George Shibley?

HARRY. I am *trying* to get him to understand who we are. Until he gets us, he will never be able to represent Dale!

RUDI. *(Keeps massaging.)* We're lucky to have George. A well respected attorney with a good name —

HARRY. I'm surprised you're defending him, he's an Arab.

RUDI. He's quite good-looking. He IS one of them, right?

HARRY. Definitely. I have finally figured out how to tell the difference: by smell. Hetero-men have a distinctly unpleasant odor.

RUDI. Are you *sure* you're the right man to be working with George?

HARRY. *I'm* not the problem! He is. And if he can't fully come along to our way of thinking, he's out. We'll find someone just as good! *(Rudi is silent. Stops massaging. Suddenly it dawns on Harry.)* I'm a tornado, aren't I? *(Rudi says nothing.)* Fine, you deal with George.

RUDI. If you insist. *(Now he continues to massage.)*

HARRY. Meet with him tomorrow.

RUDI. *Ja* … uh … I'll have to reschedule. Tomorrow I meet once more with Nigel Butler.

HARRY. Once more?

RUDI. *(A little nervous.)* He's approached me about possibly joining his shop next year.

HARRY. *(Taken aback.)* Well, damn. Uh — Congratulations! When did this happen?

RUDI. The other day.

HARRY. Why the hell didn't you tell me right away? *(Rudi is silent.)* His company is in New York. Would he expect you to move there?

RUDI. *(Steely.)* I am determined to be very successful in this country.

HARRY. *(Surprised at the rawness of that statement. It's not like Rudi.)* I know you will be.

RUDI. He also wants me to be married. Or at least to go straight.

HARRY. What about us?

RUDI. *(Equally steely.)* I am determined for that to continue as well.
HARRY. I left my wife to be with you. Gave up the Communist Party. *(Beat. They're both silent.)* I wish I could crack your skull open — *(Clarifying.)* and read your mind.
RUDI. *(Torn.)* Actually … so do I. *(Rudi exits. Lights shift to a secondhand store. Dale and Harry stand near racks or piles of clothes. Harry flips through the men's jackets and suits. Dale seems decidedly uncomfortable.)*
DALE. *(In the middle of a conversation.)* It doesn't matter.
HARRY. *(Lowering his voice.)* Being — "that way" — is already two strikes against you. But looking good in a suit — *might* just take away a strike … Which do you like?
DALE. Doesn't matter.
HARRY. Dale Jennings has an opinion about everything. I know you've got an opinion about a damn suit! *(Dale shrugs. Harry's puzzled. Looks through suits.)* Okay. You could go for this loose-fitting jacket — with pronounced shoulders. *Esquire* labeled it "the bold look."
DALE. *(Covering.)* Oh yeah, right. I remember reading that.
HARRY. *(Catching on to Dale's lack of knowledge about suits.)* … Or a double-breasted jacket. With a — *(Harry looks incorrectly at the bottom of the jacket.)* Is this a notched lapel or a peaked one?
DALE. *(Inspecting bottom of the jacket.)* Uh … peaked.
HARRY. Yes, it *is* peaked. But this — *(Folded flap on top part of jacket.)* is the lapel.
DALE. Big deal. You found out my dirty little secret. I've never even worn a suit before. My girlfriends always told me what to buy. Just tell me!
HARRY. This is your first suit. It's important you get something that YOU like. Look around. *(Dale starts looking at the different suits. Harry does the same. But then Harry stops. In the middle of the rack it switches to women's clothes. He looks at gowns, robes. Then spots at the end an extremely long white shawl. On a whim he takes it off the rack. Slips it on. Although he still looks extremely masculine, there's something about the way he flips the shawl over his shoulder that gives a hint of femininity. Surprises and pleases Harry.)*
DALE. What are you doing? You're not that kind of a … Are you?
HARRY. Try it on once — it pigeonholes you forever? Maybe — *just* today — I want to sit in Mother's chair and wear her shawl. *(A gruff store employee [played by Man #1] approaches.)*
MAN #1. Excuse me, sir, but what you're wearing —

HARRY. I intend to pay for.
MAN #1. I never doubted that. It's just that it's a woman's shawl.
HARRY. *(Blurting out.)* I'm homosexual, not blind! *(Man is shocked. He tightens. Man looks to Dale for reinforcements.)*
DALE. *(Nervous.)* … Don't look to *me* for help. I'm in *his* camp. *(Dale and Harry stand as a unit. Store Employee glares, then backs down.)*
MAN #1. *(Uneasy.)* Well … when you're ready to make a purchase … *(Man #1 strides offstage.)*
HARRY. *(Stunned.)* That's the first time I ever let the mask fall in front of "one of them."
DALE. *(Nervous.)* Did you see how nervous he got?
HARRY. *(Like a teacher.)* Do you know why?
DALE. In school, I hated being called on. *(Thinks it over.)* Because we stood together?
HARRY. Thanks. *(Lights shift to … the courtroom. An anxious Bob, Chuck, and Rudi enter together. Sit down. Dale enters in his brand new suit, proud of it, but nervous. He sits further in front of the men, very much alone. Harry follows wearing his shawl. He's a bit anxious with it on, but tries not to let it show. He sits. The other three stare at the shawl, stunned. Rudi looks around at other people watching this. Chuck continues to stare at Harry wearing his shawl. Finally …)*
CHUCK. Why are you wearing that shawl?
HARRY. I intend *never* to be mistaken for heterosexual again … Besides, I like the way it feels. Draping my body. Caressing it. *(Concerned.)* Think it looks good on me?
CHUCK. … Not really.
RUDI. It's like we are in a cage at a zoo. Everyone's gawking at us.
BOB. *(Nervous, but oddly getting off on this situation.)* Can you blame them? We're sitting behind the defendant. It's rare to see a bright-tailed homosexual-bird out in broad daylight. Which species is this one?
CHUCK. *(To cover his nerves, trying to be funny.)* A *cock*-atoo.
RUDI. *(Not pleased.)* And behind him, the peacock. *(Re: Harry's shawl.)* With his colorful wingspan.
HARRY. *(Since he's being goaded.)* Shall I open up my plumage?
RUDI. No! This is Dale's trial. Not *The Harry Hay Show.*
CHUCK. *(Seeing people looking at them.)* I knew this was dangerous for Dale, but …
BOB. You okay?

CHUCK. Does that man have a camera?
RUDI. *Sheisse,* does he?
HARRY. *(Watching Dale, like a proud father.)* … Even if Dale loses, one good thing will come out of this horrendous situation: look at the way Dale feels wearing his first suit. *(Harry stands, goes to a nervous Dale and reassuredly taps him on the back.)* Suit looks good.
DALE. *(Trying to convince himself.)* I'm gonna be fine … *(Finally seeing Harry's get-up, surprised.)* Nice shawl.
HARRY. You mean it?
DALE. Uh … sure. *(During this, Bob stands and becomes George Shibley.)*
GEORGE. Members of the jury, good morning. My father always told me — you learn the most from difficult or uncomfortable situations. Today we have one of those — because my client is a homosexual. *(We feel the temperature of the room change. Rudi studies the shaken and uncomfortable jury.)* But that does not mean he isn't a good man. A good American. *(During the above, Rudi lightly coughs.)*
RUDI. Sorry. *(As George continues speaking, Rudi grows more uneasy. Is probably having a panic attack. But trying to mask it.)*
GEORGE. The only pervert here — the arresting officer. Who perverted the codes of decency.
RUDI. *(Stands, to Harry.) Entschuldigung.* [Excuse me.] *(Rudi gets up and goes to the back.)*
GEORGE. Thinking he could entrap a man who would be too frightened to fight back. *(In the back, Rudi tries to remain unobtrusive. Calm his nerves. George's speech does a time jump.)* At this time, I'd like to call up Officer Clark. *(Lights dim and a bright, ominous searchlight shines on Rudi. He tries not to freak out. But does, nonetheless.)* Do you know the expression "NHI," Officer Clark? It's short for "No Humans Involved." A quaint old police term for a crime involving someone who's just a lowlife. Or black. Or Latino. In your report, next to Mr. Jennings' name, I see *you've* written NHI. No Humans Involved. That *is* your handwriting, isn't it? … No further questions. *(George exits offstage. Then lights come up on the trial — now long over. Rudi returns to his seat, joining the others.)*
HARRY. *(Concerned.)* What's wrong? If you're feeling sick, you should go home. Are you?
RUDI. Yes.
HARRY. Then let's go —
RUDI. And no.

HARRY. Can't be both.
RUDI. *(Confused.)* My brain wants to be here, but my neck, then my face. Like it's on fire.
HARRY. *(Complimenting him.)* And still you're here.
CHUCK. *(To Rudi and Harry, interrupting, optimistic.)* The jury. I couldn't stop staring at them They looked almost — sympathetic.
RUDI. Or were they putting up *their* mask?
CHUCK. *(His pessimistic side kicking in.)* My thoughts, exactly. *(Harry sees Dale sitting there, so alone. Harry starts towards him.)*
RUDI. What are you doing?
HARRY. Sitting next to him.
RUDI. But — you're not the defendant. *(Ignoring Rudi, Harry goes to an anxious Dale. Sits next to him. For a moment puts his hand on Dale's arm. Then stops. Chuck — though nervous — gets up, stands by Dale. Rudi remains in his seat.)*
DALE. *(Somewhat out of it, to Chuck.)* How did it go?
CHUCK. What?
DALE. The trial.
CHUCK. *(Puzzled.)* You were here, too.
DALE. *(Couldn't concentrate.)* Yeah, but I just … I couldn't — I just kept thinking "What if the jury turns on me — 'cuz of George's snooty accent?" *(Turning back to Rudi.)* That's crazy. Don't you think, Rudi?
RUDI. Being judged by your accent? Ridiculous. *(All laugh. Still Rudi doesn't join them upfront. George reenters.)*
GEORGE. It's a hung jury. One juror's holding out.
RUDI. For?
GEORGE. Guilty.
CHUCK. *(Honestly surprised.)* The other eleven believed Dale?
HARRY. Truth is a very powerful thing.
CHUCK. I know, but … I know!
GEORGE. The judge is completely dismissing the case. AND — the prosecutor doesn't think he can win this a second time.
DALE. *(Still confused.)* I see.
GEORGE. It's over. You've won. Congratulations. *(George — a bit awkwardly — shakes Dale's hand and starts to exit.)*
HARRY. *(To George.)* Not so fast, George. We're going out to celebrate.
GEORGE. You should. You've won an important case.
HARRY. So have you.

GEORGE. *(Truthful.)* Your shawl, Mr. Hay, is so bright. It makes me — uncomfortable. Good on you. *(George exits. Harry's oddly pleased by George's comment. Reassured.)*
DALE. *(Exhausted, relieved.)* I'm free?
RUDI. As a cockatoo.
CHUCK. That was *my* joke.
BOB. *(Reentering.)* Just heard the newsflash from Shibley. And I gave him a big hug … So who is ready to lose this dump and get some liquid joy? Martinis on Bob.
CHUCK. At 10 A.M.?
BOB. … Margaritas on Bob?
DALE. I haven't exactly slept much. I should get home. Get some shut-eye. But tonight?
HARRY. And — I bought a new shawl for the occasion. Magenta.
RUDI. *Ach was!* … *(Covering.)* You sure that's your color?
BOB. What are *you* wearing, Rudi?
RUDI. … I need to work tonight.
HARRY. Since when?
RUDI. With Vincente. It came up suddenly. *(Rudi exits.)*
CHUCK. *(Excited about an idea.)* This is big — this win. The publicity we're going to get … we can use to raise money *(Explaining to Harry.)* — to pay for other lawyers —
HARRY. *(Catching on, finishes Chuck's sentence.)* — Taking on similar cases! Good idea. *(Harry exits.)*
CHUCK. I know! *(Chuck exits. Only Bob and Dale are left onstage.)*
BOB. Go home. Treat yourself to a long sleep. A good bath. Or … *(Re: Dale's scar.)* This scar still looks awful — ly appealing.
DALE. … Ya dump me. I feel lousy. Go to a men's room. Almost do something. Don't. Get arrested anyway! Go to trial all 'cuz of — *(Points to Bob.)* And NOW you got the nerve to ask me —
BOB. *(Interrupting.)* Well you seem different. More in control. *(Whispering.)* I think it's the suit.
DALE. Bob, do you even remotely know how pathetic you come off?! Do you?! … I would never ever date you again. *(Dale exits. Bob stands there, blank. Not revealing anything. Then.)*
BOB. *(Glib.)* Well who said I wanted to *date* you! *(Bob stands there. Alone. Then the lights shift to … The Chuckwagon. Bob races in, calling out to those in the diner. Dale and Harry, wearing his magenta shawl and a Robin Hood-like hat, enter. Chuck enters as well, but separately. In his own thoughts. To audience.)* Hey every-

one, eleven to one for acquittal. The world cares about us! You at the Chuckwagon care about us!
HARRY. It's historic. Because of you, Dale. Your bravery.
DALE. *(Shrugging it off.)* Bravery? Any of you guys woulda done the same thing … Right?
HARRY. *(Questioning.)* I'd like to think so —
BOB. Of course we would've. Well, except maybe Rudi. *(As Bob laughs —)*
HARRY. *(Pissed off.)* Bob — not even a little bit funny.
BOB. Why is everyone picking on sweet, funny — ? *(To Chuck, picking on him.) You're* awfully silent. I'm surprised. Usually you're the first to jump in with a nasty —
CHUCK. *(Quiet.)* I've been looking through the newspapers. Including the evening editions. Not one story about our case.
DALE. Impossible. This is a big victory.
CHUCK. It's a deliberate conspiracy of silence. We've been shut out.
HARRY. You checked all the papers? *(Chuck glares at Harry.)* I'm sure you did.
CHUCK. They don't like to discuss us. We make them uncomfortable.
DALE. *(Disagreeing.)* No … *They* don't think we deserve to be talked about in "proper" company. We could've burned down a church at high noon on Sunday and they wouldn't have printed it. 'Cuz we're just a bunch of queers.
BOB. *(Can't quite take it in.)* So — no one's ever going to know about our victory?
CHUCK. *(To himself.)* It's over for the Matttachine Society.
BOB. You *really* know how to bring down a party, Chuck. THAT is why I stopped dating you. I can't handle a downer spirit in my life. You hear me?!
HARRY. Okay, okay. The papers didn't print our story. There has *got* to be a way to get the word out. At least to other Temperamentals.
CHUCK. I don't see how.
BOB. *(Annoyed at what he perceives as Chuck's pessimism.)* "I don't see how."
CHUCK. *(On edge.)* Well it's not like we have our own newspapers — or radio stations. So how do we do it, Bob?!
BOB. *(Disgusted with Chuck, quietly sings/mutters to himself. Sung to the melody of "God Save the Queen.")*

GOD SAVE US NELLY QUEENS, GOD SAVE —

HARRY. THAT — is how we're going to send the news out there.
DALE. *(Sarcastic.)* Through Bob's singing?
HARRY. Up and down our underground railroad system.
DALE. *(Puzzled.)* I didn't know we had one.
HARRY. Are you kidding? We've got the greatest musical underground in the world. We're just not taking advantage of it and passing the word along. Don't you get it?
BOB. *(Considers, then.)* ... No.
HARRY. *(Mimicking Steinbeck's* Grapes of Wrath.*)* Wherever there's Standing Room in the back of an opera house ... we are there ... Wherever there's a seedy motel piano bar with cheap liquor and married men — from out of town —
DALE. *(Remaining pseudo-serious, mimicking* Grapes of Wrath.*)* We — are — there.
CHUCK. Whenever the pastor of a church begs his congregation for a few more tenors to join the choir —
ALL. We — are — there!
HARRY. *(Sings as Bob races offstage.)*
FROM EVERY MOUNTAINSIDE
DALE.
LONG MAY WE LIVE AND DIE
HARRY, DALE and CHUCK.
GOD SAVE US —
(Whispering.)
NELLY QUEENS
(Loud again.)
GOD SAVE US —
(Bob reenters playing on his clarinet (or recorder) the opening melody of "God Save the Queen." As he continues playing, lights shift and we find ourselves in an underground meeting room as our other four guys sing and dance to Bob's playing. Each of them finding their "nelly queen.")
DALE, HARRY, RUDI and CHUCK.
FROM EVERY MOUNTAINSIDE
LONG MAY WE LIVE AND DIE
GOD SAVE US NELLY QUEENS
GOD SAVE US QUEENS
(Applause. As a tearful Harry — in his shawl — speaks to the crowd, Dale stands next to him. The others perhaps begin handing out fliers to the audience.)
HARRY. *(Once again tearing up.)* There goes my sprinkler system

again … What a privilege, standing in front of you. Know what I love about our little congregation? WE … can carry a tune. *(Pointing specifically at someone.)* Most of us … Take a look at the literature we're handing out. I know it seems bold, branching out to other cities. But after our success with Dale's case — *(To Dale.)* How's it feel to be our poster boy?

DALE. I certainly didn't ask for it, but now —

HARRY. *(Interrupting.)* Great speech you gave earlier. Short. To the point. *(To audience.)* And after our success with Dale's case, there's real hope. For change … Bob? *(Harry looks to Bob, who joins them.)*

BOB. *(Looks up at the lighting guy.)* Could you bump up the lights a little more? Thank you … And now, *our* benediction. *(Our five guys get in the middle of the audience and take people's hands. Bob sincerely speaks to "the crowd.")* Our interlocking and protecting hands guarantee that we are united together for an immense — yet simple purpose.

HARRY. *(To audience.)* We are resolved that our people will find security — and equality of rights — in tomorrow's world.

DALE. *(Personal.)* You are the brave ones. The pioneers. The first in the United States to gather in a public place like this.

CHUCK. We swear that from now on — no boy or girl need make this crossing alone — afraid — and in the dark — ever again.

RUDI. To do that, we must dedicate ourselves to each other. Aware of the immense significance of our allegiance.

HARRY. That ends our meeting.

BOB. *(To someone in crowd, whispers, teasing.)* You can let go of my hand now. *(Our guys start straightening up. Basking in the glow of the moment. Bob still flirts with the person whose hand he held. To Chuck.)* I love the benediction.

CHUCK. You always say that.

BOB. Well … I always love it.

HARRY. The whole night went perfectly … Well … *(Looks to Dale.)*

DALE. What?

HARRY. You forgot. Again. *(Off Dale's puzzlement.)* To say that we're a sexual minority.

DALE. Oh right. *(Fessing up.)* I didn't forget.

HARRY. *(Puzzled.)* You didn't?

DALE. I've been doing a lot of — deep thinking —

HARRY. Deep thinking?

DALE. — and have decided —
BOB. *(Interrupting, helping out.)* — Actually we *all* decided. That it's better to leave that phrase out: Sexual minority.
RUDI. What do you mean "all"? No one asked *me*.
BOB. *(Casually.)* Well if you were around more —
HARRY. *(To Bob and Dale, hurt.)* Wait. So the three of you went behind our backs — ?
CHUCK. *(Jumping in, taking control.)* The problem is, some of the newer members don't like being thought of as a minority. In an inferior position.
BOB. They don't wanna be "Negroes."
DALE. For christsake, Bob!
BOB. What? Even Negroes don't want to be Negroes!
CHUCK. Yes, Bob is a bigot. But in this case he's correct. In America, we ARE second-class citizens. Like Negroes —
RUDI. Which is *exactly* why we need to tell them that we're a sexual minority.
BOB. Some of these guys *already* feel lousy about themselves. Last thing they need — a group of their *own* no less telling them *one more* depressing thing about who they are.
HARRY. So — what? They can't deal with the truth? They just want to have fun?
RUDI. *(Joining in with Harry.)* Unless everyone in the Mattachine Society understands that we're a sexual minority — and therefore second-class citizens —
HARRY. — Then we're doomed.
RUDI. Harry's concept is the foundation of our organization … It's the core of what we believe. What I thought all of you believed as well.
HARRY. *(Touched.)* … Thank you, Rudi.
DALE. We're gonna lose a few members.
HARRY. Sure, the less political ones.
CHUCK. And we're all okay with that?! Not welcoming every Temperamental into our circle?
HARRY. To hold onto our fundamental beliefs? I am.
RUDI. So am I.
DALE. *(Mulling it over.)* Well … we ARE a political organization … so losing the less political ones … *(Deciding, to Harry.)* Yeah.
HARRY. That's three for "yea." Or yeah. *(Turns to Bob.)* Bob?
BOB. *(Agreeing with Harry.)* I guess I'm not *quite* ready to give up

my pinko commie roots.
HARRY. *(Turns to Chuck.)* … It has to be unanimous. *(As Chuck considers, Harry invades his space.)*
CHUCK. Give me some room — to think! … *(Chuck moves away. Considers.)* It *would* be nice to hold on to who we are. As long as we can.
RUDI. *(Personal.)* … Yes.
HARRY. *(Off Rudi's response.)* … Yes … So it's "unanimous." Dale will continue to say that we're a sexual minority. *(Beat. Then Harry and Rudi return to straightening up the place as Bob, Dale, and Chuck exit. Harry and Rudi are left alone, piling up chairs.)*
RUDI. Nothing like a good argument …
HARRY. *(Re: the betrayal.)* I can't believe that the three of them — *(Harry tries not to think about it as they straighten up.)* Bob may love the benediction, but for *me* … The two of us — setting up. Putting away. How many hours do you think we've…?
RUDI. *(Determined.)* … Not enough.
HARRY. *(Touched.)* When you just spoke up for me — in front of the guys —
RUDI. I said it because I believe it.
HARRY. *(Heading towards Rudi.)* I know. That's why it gets me all — *(Harry romantically touches Rudi's arm. Rudi noticeably flinches.)*
RUDI. *(Startles.)* Harry!
HARRY. What? You're the one who's always insisted —
RUDI. *(Immediately back to himself.)* And still do. Sorry. Even when I'm standing on solid ground — *inside* — it's like I'm on some runaway merry-go-round. *(Rudi affectionately touches Harry.)* Feels nice. And safe. Right?
HARRY. I should hope so.
RUDI. The other day — I lied to you — when I said I was working for Vincente. *(Harry pulls away.)* You stopped touching.
HARRY. What do you mean lied —
RUDI. Please continue. Touching. *(Though agitated, Harry touches Rudi's arm again.)* Nigel Butler and his wife came to town. Took me out to dinner. Then the four of us went dancing —
HARRY. The *four* of us?
RUDI. Men found her very attractive. My date. They kept looking over at her. And then at me. All jealous. I kind of liked that. Guess what her name is? Anita. Isn't that — ridiculous? *You* lose an Anita and I —

HARRY. *(Concerned.)* Find one?
RUDI. Of course not! I couldn't even kiss her good night. I thought I'd be cheating on you.
HARRY. Not even on the cheek?
RUDI. No. And *I* am European … Not even on the cheek. *(Rudi kisses Harry on the cheek.)* One other thing.
HARRY. *(Still uneasy.)* I'm listening.
RUDI. Right now, at this moment, I don't think I've ever felt closer to you. *(Man #3, playing a different character, enters in a fedora.)*
MAN #3. *(To Rudi, abrupt.)* Harry Hay.
RUDI. What do you want?
MAN #3. Harry Hay.
HARRY. *(Moving towards him, extends hand.)* And you are — *(Man #3 pulls out an envelope, places it in Harry's hand, and exits. As Harry opens it, Rudi stands over him. They both read it. Shaken.)*
RUDI. *(Nervous, but trying to reassure Harry.)* I'm here. *(As Bob's clarinet is heard playing the first two bars of the melody of "Alas I'm Quite Certain that Love is Truly Blind," Harry moves away and sits by himself. In another area Rudi paces. While in another area, Bob enters as he finishes playing.)*
BOB. *(To an entering Dale.)* Now sing it back.
DALE.

ALAS I'M QUITE CERTAIN THAT —

(Can't remember it.) Maybe that's a sign.
BOB. We already agreed. Until Harry gets back, someone needs to sing his part.
DALE. C'mon, it's *his* song … The new members don't even give a damn we got our name from "the Société Mattachine."
BOB. They may not care about a lot of things, but they *all* love a man in a wig. That's me. And I am NOT giving it up!
DALE. *(Whispering, looking around.)* … Yesterday, a new member pulls me aside, shows me the *Herald-Express* — this list of people who gotta testify before the House Un-American Activities Committee —
BOB. *(Knows, finishes Dale's sentence.)* — and he saw Harry's name.
DALE. *(Whispering.)* Kid starts flipping out, saying — "if Harry's a commie, we could all be arrested!"
BOB. *("Acting" stunned.)* A scared nelly queen — call AP and UPI! Study your lyric sheet.
DALE. *(Still whispering.)* You don't get it. He wasn't just scared, he

was angry —
BOB. Why are you whispering? This is the one place we're safe. Let's take it from the top … Actually, I overheard some other guys squawking about that article. I said, "What's the big deal? I was a commie as well." That shut 'em up. They just looked at me like — like I was Esther the leper! Think I said too much?
DALE. *(Unsure.)* Ya told the truth.
BOB. Oh dear. *(Off Dale's puzzlement.)* Whenever Bob starts "speaking truth," it messes everything up. I mean like with us! Just when I think my real life is finally starting, I always do something to … Why is that?
DALE. Jeez, Bob, why are you asking *me? (Dale exits. Bob, alone, begins to slowly play the opening melancholy melody of "Turnip." Lights down on him. He exits as lights up on … Rudi and Vincente Minnelli enter. They're on a deserted soundstage.)*
RUDI. *(Finishing the thought, "Harry's in D.C. …)* And *I'm* here. I'm here.
VINCENTE. Bravo.
RUDI. *(Not amused.)* He flew all the way to D.C. By himself.
VINCENTE. And the alternative? You by his side — while the House Un-American Activities Committee grills him. Reporters, everywhere — wondering — "Who is that man with Harry Hay?"
RUDI. *(Conflicted.)* Why do you think I am *here.*
VINCENTE. *(Looking around, his version of "home.")* … Shhh … I love the silence of an empty soundstage. So alive — with possibilities.
RUDI. Alive? It's empty.
VINCENTE. … I am directing Oscar Levant, Cyd Charisse, and Fred Astaire. Could life be any better than that? And when did this — what I think of as my real life — truly kick into high gear? When I married. At the age of 42. I was finally "respectable." Marrying — best decision I ever made … for my career. Take the job in New York with Nigel Butler.
RUDI. And get married? What of love?
VINCENTE. You'll be fine. One piece of advice: never look back. It's a waste of — *(Sharply biting the inside of his mouth.)* — Mmmm! Ow … Perhaps the mouth knows something *I* don't. If you really want to go to D.C., go. Be with Harry. *(Rudi doesn't move. Vincente's intrigued.)* Go.
RUDI. But I asked you here so you would stop me.

VINCENTE. We *are* kindred spirits. Well, mostly. How do you do it? Being out in public with Harry. That shawl.
RUDI. You should see his hats. *(Thinking about them.) Herr — lich. (Off Vincente's puzzlement.)* It means delightful. *(As Rudi thinks about Harry and his hats, Vincente watches on. Sees how much Rudi loves Harry.)* I have to go to Washington.
VINCENTE. *(Understands and yet.)* Be careful, Rudi. You are so talented. *(Vincente exits. Rudi paces, lost in thought, then finally makes HIS decision. He strides over and joins Harry at a heterosexual bar/restaurant in Washington, D.C. Harry's in a suit and wears his magenta shawl over it. He's extremely anxious.)*
RUDI. *(Appears cool, comforting.)* I still don't think it's discrimination.
HARRY. *(Anxious.)* Then explain to me why other people have bar nuts and we don't?!
RUDI. We have a lousy waiter.
HARRY. No waiter, no lawyer. Doesn't seem to be my year. All those great liberal attorneys, rushing to handle communists and socialists. But the minute I told them I formed the Mattachine Society — not even *one* of them — ! Although what the hell could a lawyer do in this case anyway?
RUDI. Be there for you.
HARRY. That's why you're here — *(With an edge.)* finally.
RUDI. … Were you surprised when I arrived?
HARRY. I knew you'd be here. You're an honorable man.
RUDI. And if you lose and they slam you in jail, I'll be there for you, too!
HARRY. I know you will. But if I win —
RUDI. I will be there.
HARRY. … Is it warm in here?
RUDI. Take off your shawl. If you're warm.
HARRY. I bet you'd like that, wouldn't you?
RUDI. What?
HARRY. Sometimes, I get the feeling you don't appreciate my newfound sense of style. Especially when I wear — or god forbid — open up my plumage — right in the middle of a hetero establishment. *(Harry begins to open up his shawl/plumage.)*
RUDI. What are you doing?
HARRY. *(His plumage opening wider.)* There's a Negro poet — Jean Toomer — *so* light-skinned he could pass for white. And many times did — because he could. Which I get. I passed for

years. But now it hurts too much and I WON'T goddamn do it, Rudi! I won't goddamn —
RUDI. Harry, lower your shawl! *(Harry does.)* I know you're upset about the trial tomorrow —
HARRY. You're lucky. You can still pass.
RUDI. *(Enraged.)* Excuse me, but I have *never* been lucky when it comes to — ! In Vienna, it didn't matter how "non-Jewish" one looked. The government knew our lineage. My family couldn't pass and half of them died because of it! Now here in the United States — bloodlines do not betray one's inner — nature. So finally I pass. And I hate it. Because now *I'm* the one who must choose *between* — *(Pause.)* I hate it.
HARRY. *(Seeing the pain Rudi's in.)* I know.
RUDI. I hate it! *(Harry realizes he needs to let Rudi go for both of their sakes.)*
HARRY. Together, we created a political movement, a great accomplishment.
RUDI. *Ja.*
HARRY. But now, we don't need you as a leader. Move to New York, become successful —
RUDI. Move to New —
HARRY. So when the time is right, we'll have money. Influence. Because in the USA, the poor can't change things.
RUDI. I told you that from the beginning!
HARRY. You need to go.
RUDI. It's something I'll definitely consider —
HARRY. No, you need to go now. It's too dangerous for you to stay.
RUDI. I flew all the way to D.C. I am not —
HARRY. I will make an even bigger scene —
RUDI. Go ahead —
HARRY. *(Speaking louder.)* I can see it splashed in the papers! "Harry Hay, communist — and homosexual — created a disturbance last evening in the presence of costume designer Rudi Gernreich, Rudi —
RUDI. All right! All right ! *(Rudi stands. Perhaps his action even surprises him.)* The terrible thing about *all* of this?
HARRY. What?
RUDI. I actually love your plumage ... *And* magenta. *(Harry stands.)* Good luck, tomorrow. *(Rudi starts to hug Harry goodbye.*

Harry stops him — puts out his hand.) A handshake?
HARRY. Good luck to us both. *(The two men clasp hands together. Fearful — of the unknown. Rudi heads out. Then stops. Wants to turn back. But remembers Vincente's admonishment not to. Rudi exits. Harry stands alone, trying to remain strong as — Bob enters with his clarinet and Chuck enters carrying in a box. Bob plays the first two introductory bars of "Turnip." Which is interrupted by a recorded voice.)*
RECORDED VOICE. "Are you now or have you EVER been — *(Note: not going any further than "ever been" in the quote. As Bob plays the next two introductory bars of "Turnip," at the same time Harry starts to head out to his trial. But stops as he catches himself in the mirror. Wearing his shawl. He looks at it. Admires it. But also knows if he even remotely hopes to win, he can't wear it.)* "Are you now or have you ever been." *(With great difficulty, Harry slowly lets his shawl drop from his body. As if he's shedding his skin. A skin he had fallen in love with. At the same time, Dale pulls the wig out of the box and proudly places this "skin" on Bob's head. An anxious Harry heads out to his HUAC trial. Harry's hit with a harsh light. We see his entire body language change. Becoming more "masculine." Less "temperamental." He even speaks in a more "masculine" way. Except it slips when he says "Cousins at Plymouth — ")*
HARRY. I am a 15th-generation American, Mr. Tavener. Going back to 1608. "Cousins at Plymouth — " *(Making that phrase and his body language more masculine.)* "Cousins at Plymouth Rock." My father was a partner of Herbert Hoover —
RECORDED VOICE. Fascinating. But *are* you a member of the Communist Party?
HARRY. Uh … No. I'm not a member. *(Pound of the gavel. A stunned Harry turns away and sits. Then three harsh separate lights shine down. Bob, Dale, and Chuck step into them. They're also being grilled one-on-one — but by new Mattachine members.)*
NEW MATTACHINE MEMBER. *(Voiceover.)* Fascinating. But *was* Harry a member of the Communist Party?
DALE. *(Uneasy, to an audience member.)* … Yeah, he was.
BOB. *(Nervous to admit this, to a different audience member.)* … Of course he was.
CHUCK. *(Answering a different question, to a third audience member.)* Calm down. I heard you. *(Imitating one of them.)* "If Harry is a communist, they'll think we're *all* activists." Although I hate to break it to you, but you *are* activists. And by the way — I was *also*

a member of the Party.
BOB. *(To more audience members.)* We ALL were. Do you *actually* think a radical organization is born from moderate people?!
CHUCK. *(Also to more audience members.)* I understand. Our "leftist leanings" make you a little nervous. But that's no reason for you to drop out.
DALE. You are not dropping out. Do you hear me?
BOB. We're more than just a political organization —
CHUCK. We're a Brotherhood. *(Realizing.)* A family. Why would you want to leave that?
DALE. Think it over first.
BOB. Let's sit down. Talk things — wait!
CHUCK. If you'd just let me explain — Don't go … Don't. *(But the new members have gone. Our trio looks to each other, understanding that their world is shaking. And realizing what they must do. Lights back up on Harry.)*
HARRY. *(Morose, quietly.)* They were supposed to ask "are you now or have you *ever* been?" But they only asked "are you *now?*" And of course —
CHUCK. *(Quickly pieces it together.)* You had left the Communist Party over a year ago!
HARRY. So it got dismissed. On a technicality. Isn't that … ridiculous.
BOB. That is beautiful Harry! … Right?
HARRY. *(Heartbroken.)* I took off my shawl.
DALE. Huh?
HARRY. Rudi, he's moved to New York … Well — at least *here* — I'm home. *(Dale is silent, not exactly sure if that's true anymore.)* What?
DALE. *(Not dealing with that.)* I'm sorry about Rudi.
HARRY. What is going on?! *(And as Harry waits for Dale to speak, Chuck and Bob move towards Harry. Dale, Bob, and Chuck stand together facing him.)* Men.
CHUCK. *(Chosen to start this.)* Your politics — *(Correcting himself.)* *Our* politics. They're scaring the hell out of the newer members.
HARRY. *(Uncertain.)* I see.
DALE. We're losing them, a lot of them.
HARRY. Then they're out. As previously agreed. I mean if they're not political enough —
BOB. *(Interrupting, anxious.)* What is more important? Us? Or the

organization staying together?!

HARRY. … Oh I see … Us? Or the organization? A few months ago — during one of our ceremonies, a young man whispered in my ear: "Thank you for my life." Every time I think about that, it wipes me out.

DALE. That was a few months ago. They ain't thanking us now.

BOB. Chuck has the solution, Harry.

HARRY. *(To Chuck, not pleased.)* … And what is the solution, Chuck?

CHUCK. The four of us dissolve the original board and hand over the Mattachine name. That way, the organization can continue.

HARRY. Without *us?* The commies and rebels who started it?

CHUCK. It's not about us.

HARRY. *(Exploding.)* You are all striking me down! This is like a physical blow.

DALE. It's not about you.

HARRY. I'm the one with the original vision: to develop a highly ethical homosexual culture!

BOB. And they just want to fit in.

HARRY. They'll never fit in, Bob! They'll never fit in!

CHUCK. *(Quietly, firmly.)* We have to do this. For the good of the organization.

BOB. We've always been unanimous on all our votes. So when we resign —

DALE. — It's also gotta be unanimous.

CHUCK. What do you say, Harry? For the good of the Mattachine Society.

HARRY. *(Still furious and hurt.)* First answer me one question. Is it that easy for the three of you to walk away from our baby? To just give it up?! … Well?

DALE. Being your poster boy has been so much damn work. And responsibility. That I never thought I could do … It's been an honor trying.

BOB. *(Serious.)* These last three years — *this* — has been the only thing that's excited me enough to get up each morning. *(This statement surprises the others.)*

CHUCK. I am a philosophical pessimist. But a glandular optimist. So while I sometimes worried that the organization *might* fall apart, I never thought it would *actually* — *(Pause.)* And now that it's about to — *(Chuck gets too emotional to speak anymore.)*

HARRY. That's all I wanted to hear. Cuz it's killing me, too. It's killing me … Well, if it has to be unanimous …
CHUCK. Yes?
HARRY. We need Rudi as well.
BOB. But he's in New York.
HARRY. We need Rudi. We all have to stand in front of that convention — and resign — together.
CHUCK. It's just the four of us. Make it unanimous, Harry. *(Harry considers. And considers. Then finally joins them. Lights shift. We hear a strange sort of Liberty Bell sounding — for it has a cracked or hollow sound. The four founding fathers reluctantly stand in front of the convention. Thunderous applause.)*
BOB. *(As they bow, whispering to each other.)* Sure, now that they've won, they love us!
HARRY. Screw them.
DALE. *(Under his breath.)* Small-minded little chickenshits.
CHUCK. *(His held-down rage finally coming up.)* No, sissies. God damn … sissies! Every … fucking … faggoty one of them! *(Light flash — as if a picture's being taken. All freeze. Then Harry speaks, still angry.)*
HARRY. *(To audience.)* That was one of the few pictures taken of us. It was too dangerous. After our "glorious" resignation, the L.A. Mattachine Society continued on without us — turning into a frivolous social organization and was then forgotten. All gay activism is thought to have started in 1969 at Stonewall. Well, B.S.! — *before* Stonewall — an even braver bunch of us stood up to the plate — before there even was a plate! … Chuck Rowland. Who started an organization similar to the Mattachine Society.
CHUCK. But more religious. Called the Church of One Brotherhood. But we just couldn't get enough people … *(Disappointed in people.)* People. To stand and —
HARRY. *(Interrupting.)* It didn't last. He moved back to Minnesota. Taught college drama until he retired. But then — in the early '80s — he returned to Los Angeles. Helped form a theater company dedicated to examining the "temperamental" experience.
CHUCK. We searched for a name. A positive one. *(Dawns on him.)* The *Celebration* Theater. *(Pleased something of his lasted.)* It's still around.
HARRY. Dale Jennings. Who wrote for a revolutionary new magazine called *ONE Magazine — The Homosexual Viewpoint.* But

eventually he needed to make some real money and worked as a promoter for — well —

DALE. The Ice Capades. I'm not embarrassed. Became pretty damn wealthy 'cuz of it.

HARRY. Bob Hull.

CHUCK. My Bob.

DALE. And mine.

CHUCK. *(Still a touchy subject.)* I had him first. *(Quiet pride.)* And longest.

HARRY. Bob dropped out of politics. Instead, he concentrated on having a lot of hot love affairs. Bob got older, but tried to remain young. Didn't want to let go of his boyishness. See, back *then,* you were either cute or over the hill.

BOB. When you reach that kind of a mid-life crisis. And then pour alcohol over it …

HARRY. One spring night, Bob brought home potassium cyanide. Then turned on the TV — started getting drunk — until he could face taking the cyanide. It took effect quickly. He died May 1, 1962.

CHUCK. *(To Bob, still confused over why he did it.)* I know everyone has a right to end his life. But *why,* Bob? *(Bob glares at him. He thinks Chuck knew why.)*

HARRY. The most visible and famous of our group is a man I always referred to as — Mister X. *(Rudi enters. Harry doesn't look at him. It's too difficult.)* In December 1967, he made the cover of *Time* magazine. They called him groundbreaking. Freeing women from constrictive 1950s clothing. *(Looking at his suit, an idea beginning.)* Huh. Constrictive …

RUDI. I was *so* famous, I even appeared on an episode of the television show *Batman.* Most knew me for inventing the topless bathing suit. The bottom half was conservative, basic black, while the top half was, well, a string.

HARRY. A bold statement on a classic pattern. That was Rudi. Today, his topless bathing suit hangs in the Costume Collection in the Metropolitan Museum of Art. They call him a "fashion activist."

RUDI. Activist. I loved that term. *(Still concerned he wasn't political enough and had let Harry and himself down.)* I hope it was true. Was it? … Harry? *(Harry — still not entirely over Rudi and what happened — ignores the question. Continues with "the speech.")*

HARRY. Till the day he died, I never gave away his identity. For over thirty years, it was a secret that Rudi Gernreich was one of the

/ two original —
RUDI. *(Interrupting, hurt/angry, reminding Harry of this fact.)* ONE OF THE TWO ORIGINAL FOUNDING MEMBERS OF THE MATTACHINE SOCIETY!
HARRY. … Rudi.
RUDI. Yes, Harry?
HARRY. Some things … For some reason …
RUDI. Yes?
HARRY. … You never really get over.
RUDI. *(Still unresolved.)* … Or completely understand. *(They look at each other. It feels good. But painful. Finally Rudi breaks the moment, turns back to the audience.)* For twenty years, Harry Hay searched for a place where he could — well — be heard. Belong. Then one day it finally dawned on him … No such place existed. He'd have to create that world for himself. *(During the above, Harry — in rage and frustration — has removed his clothes. He stands there — still unsure of how to channel all of his loss into something more positive. In separate areas, Dale, Bob and Chuck hold out various items of clothing. Harry points to the ones that appeal to him: a colorful button-down shirt, a pair of tight worn hippie jeans, a small dignified pair of pearls. The three guys help Harry put them on. Throughout, Rudi speaks.)* In 1979, Harry helped form an organization called the Faeries. They embrace nature. Being outsiders. Being themselves. But the name "Faeries" didn't quite work for Harry. He suggested they add another word to it: "Radical." For it is also the job of a fairy to shake up this uptight rigid world. So all Radical Faeries became front-line shock-troopers — dressing in gender-*fuck* drag. With Harry's long bright shawl … *(Rudi drapes the magenta shawl over Harry's shoulders. It's a tremendous feeling for Harry to have his old shawl covering his back once more.)* … and sun bonnet — leading the way! *(Harry stands there with great dignity as he now adds a sun bonnet. Rudi looks at it.) Herrlich* … There is no doubt that the inspiration for his clothes came from … *(Very personal — wanting to believe he contributed.)* me.
HARRY. *(Talking to the audience.)* And yes, my fellow faeries, I, too am *unfulfilled* following the driven, he-man path of the straight world. However, I am even MORE outraged at our assimilated gay brothers — who prize most the masculine, deep-voiced, "straight-acting" men! But here … there won't be any of that. Welcome "home." *(Harry puts his hands out to the audience. And*

one by one the other four place their hands out to the audience as well. So for our final moments the audience truly feel they are right in the middle of the play.) Home … Here we embrace the qualities of non-competitiveness. Creativity. *(From the heart — a now open heart, looking at many audience members.)* Don't worry, my friends, if everyone doesn't appreciate you … *(A touch of glee.)* As Jean Genet said: "Faeries are a pale and motley race that flowers in the minds of *decent* folk. Never will they be entitled to broad daylight, to real sun. But remote in these limbos, they cause curious disasters — *(Looking at the other four Mattachine members and then out at the audience — entreating them to join this new world.)* which are harbingers — of new — beauty."

End of Play

PROPERTY LIST

Battered briefcase
Several sheets of paper
Sketchbook
Black gown
Black cape
Pen
Folded piece of paper
Petition and clipboard
Blonde wig
Turnip
Phone
Ring
White shawl
Magenta shawl
Envelope
Box, containing tight hippie jeans, a colorful button-down shirt, pearls, and a sun bonnet

SOUND EFFECTS

A glass breaking or a man clearing his throat
Church bell chiming
Cocktail music
Phone ringing
F major chord
Liberty Bell sound (cracked)

(c) 2009

My Turnip

UKULELE CHORDS

MY TURNIP

)m Dm C Gm7 C
A-LAS I'M QUITE CERTAIN THAT LOVE IS TRULY BLIND

Dm Am A
E IS KINGLY – BORN OF NOBLE BIRTH

Dm Am A (one note at a time)
UT MY LOINS ACHE – FOR SOMETHING OF …. THE EARTH

Dm C
IS HEART POUNDS FOR A – TURNIP – Hee Haw!

Gm7 C
H IT'S DIRTY AND IT'S COARSE

Dm Am
YOU BITE ME, I'M BITTER (spoken) And he likes bitter.

Dm A
ND QUITE THE DOOR KIDDER

Am (forcefully) Am C Dm
HEN – SCRUBBED UP IT GLISTENS. YOU'RE CRANKY POO, I LISTEN

Am Gm7
SHE HIGH BROW? NO I AIN'T!

Am A (one note at time)
IAT'S MY (THAT'S YOUR) TURNIP

Dm C Gm7 C
JR LOVE IS PERFECTION – AND WILL RUIN MY LIFE … Huh?

Dm C Dm C
I THE BEST UPPER CLASSES – NEVER RUB WITH THE MASSES

Gm7 Am
TURNIP CANNOT BE A WIFE. … Why not?

Dm7 C D
ople will talk. And throw stones. If you *just* hadn't been a turnip!

D (loudly strumming)
IEED -- HE NEEDS – A WIFE!!

TWELVE DAYS OF CHRISTMAS

```
F        F
      FOUR CALLING BIRDS

Gm7
THREE FRENCH HENS

C
TWO TURTLE DOVES

          F              C     F
AND A PARTRIDGE IN A PEAR TREE
```

SLEEPERS, WAKE

```
   C          C                          F        C
"SLEEPERS, WAKE!"  A VOICE COMMANDS US

      C                            G                    G
AND HEED THE WORDS THAT HEAVEN HANDS US

   C         Am     G         C
AWAKE JE-RU- SALEM , AWAKE!

C             C                           F    C
MIDNIGHT'S PEACE HAS NOW BEEN BROKEN

     C                       G                G
BY URGENT SUMMONS CLEARLY SPOKEN

      C             Am          G           C
AND THUS IT'S TIME OUR PART TO TAKE
```

God Save us Nelly Queens for Clarinet or Recorder

Arrangement by Jon Marans

Turnip reprise, clarinet

Jon Maran

Page 57, Bob plays clarinet, possibly offstage, then enters

P 58, after "Jeez,Bob,why are you asking *me*?" Dale exits. Bob plays:

Recorder

Later on P 61, Bob enters and plays

Are you now or have you ever been?

Are you know or have you ever been?

Turnip reprise, recorder

Page 57, Bob plays recorder, possibly offstage, then enters

P 58, after "Jeez,Bob,why are you asking *me*?" Dale exits. Bob plays:

Later on P 61, Bob enters and plays

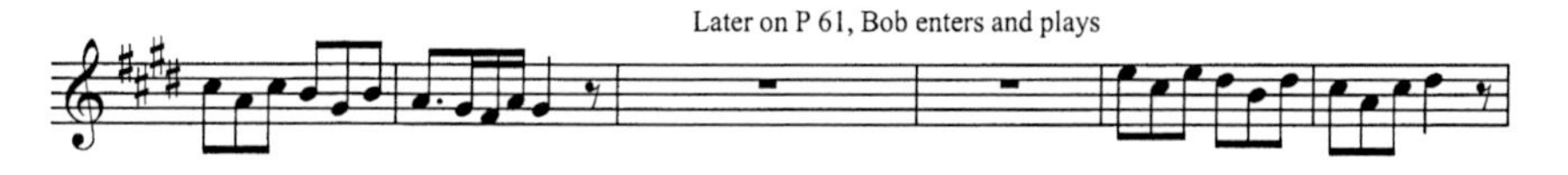

Are you now or have you ever been?

Are you now or have you ever been?

NEW PLAYS

★ **A CIVIL WAR CHRISTMAS: AN AMERICAN MUSICAL CELEBRATION by Paula Vogel, music by Daryl Waters.** It's 1864, and Washington, D.C. is settling down to the coldest Christmas Eve in years. Intertwining many lives, this musical shows us that the gladness of one's heart is the best gift of all. "Boldly inventive theater, warm and affecting." *–Talkin' Broadway.* "Crisp strokes of dialogue." *–NY Times.* [12M, 5W] ISBN: 978-0-8222-2361-0

★ **SPEECH & DEBATE by Stephen Karam.** Three teenage misfits in Salem, Oregon discover they are linked by a sex scandal that's rocked their town. "Savvy comedy." *–Variety.* "Hilarious, cliché-free, and immensely entertaining." *–NY Times.* "A strong, rangy play." *–NY Newsday.* [2M, 2W] ISBN: 978-0-8222-2286-6

★ **DIVIDING THE ESTATE by Horton Foote.** Matriarch Stella Gordon is determined not to divide her 100-year-old Texas estate, despite her family's declining wealth and the looming financial crisis. But her three children have another plan. "Goes for laughs and succeeds." *–NY Daily News.* "The theatrical equivalent of a page-turner." *–Bloomberg.com.* [4M, 9W] ISBN: 978-0-8222-2398-6

★ **WHY TORTURE IS WRONG, AND THE PEOPLE WHO LOVE THEM by Christopher Durang.** Christopher Durang turns political humor upside down with this raucous and provocative satire about America's growing homeland "insecurity." "A smashing new play." *–NY Observer.* "You may laugh yourself silly." *–Bloomberg News.* [4M, 3W] ISBN: 978-0-8222-2401-3

★ **FIFTY WORDS by Michael Weller.** While their nine-year-old son is away for the night on his first sleepover, Adam and Jan have an evening alone together, beginning a suspenseful nightlong roller-coaster ride of revelation, rancor, passion and humor. "Mr. Weller is a bold and productive dramatist." *–NY Times.* [1M, 1W] ISBN: 978-0-8222-2348-1

★ **BECKY'S NEW CAR by Steven Dietz.** Becky Foster is caught in middle age, middle management and in a middling marriage—with no prospects for change on the horizon. Then one night a socially inept and grief-struck millionaire stumbles into the car dealership where Becky works. "Gently and consistently funny." *–Variety.* "Perfect blend of hilarious comedy and substantial weight." *–Broadway Hour.* [4M, 3W] ISBN: 978-0-8222-2393-1

NEW PLAYS

★ **AT HOME AT THE ZOO by Edward Albee.** Edward Albee delves deeper into his play THE ZOO STORY by adding a first act, HOMELIFE, which precedes Peter's fateful meeting with Jerry on a park bench in Central Park. "An essential and heartening experience." *–NY Times.* "Darkly comic and thrilling." *–Time Out.* "Genuinely fascinating." *–Journal News.* [2M, 1W] ISBN: 978-0-8222-2317-7

★ **PASSING STRANGE book and lyrics by Stew, music by Stew and Heidi Rodewald, created in collaboration with Annie Dorsen.** A daring musical about a young bohemian that takes you from black middle-class America to Amsterdam, Berlin and beyond on a journey towards personal and artistic authenticity. "Fresh, exuberant, bracingly inventive, bitingly funny, and full of heart." *–NY Times.* "The freshest musical in town!" *–Wall Street Journal.* "Excellent songs and a vulnerable heart." *–Variety.* [4M, 3W] ISBN: 978-0-8222-2400-6

★ **REASONS TO BE PRETTY by Neil LaBute.** Greg really, truly adores his girlfriend, Steph. Unfortunately, he also thinks she has a few physical imperfections, and when he mentions them, all hell breaks loose. "Tight, tense and emotionally true." *–Time Magazine.* "Lively and compulsively watchable." *–The Record.* [2M, 2W] ISBN: 978-0-8222-2394-8

★ **OPUS by Michael Hollinger.** With only a few days to rehearse a grueling Beethoven masterpiece, a world-class string quartet struggles to prepare their highest-profile performance ever—a televised ceremony at the White House. "Intimate, intense and profoundly moving." *–Time Out.* "Worthy of scores of bravissimos." *–BroadwayWorld.com.* [4M, 1W] ISBN: 978-0-8222-2363-4

★ **BECKY SHAW by Gina Gionfriddo.** When an evening calculated to bring happiness takes a dark turn, crisis and comedy ensue in this wickedly funny play that asks what we owe the people we love and the strangers who land on our doorstep. "As engrossing as it is ferociously funny." *–NY Times.* "Gionfriddo is some kind of genius." *–Variety.* [2M, 3W] ISBN: 978-0-8222-2402-0

★ **KICKING A DEAD HORSE by Sam Shepard.** Hobart Struther's horse has just dropped dead. In an eighty-minute monologue, he discusses what path brought him here in the first place, the fate of his marriage, his career, politics and eventually the nature of the universe. "Deeply instinctual and intuitive." *–NY Times.* "The brilliance is in the infinite reverberations Shepard extracts from his simple metaphor." *–TheaterMania.* [1M, 1W] ISBN: 978-0-8222-2336-8

NEW PLAYS

★ **AUGUST: OSAGE COUNTY by Tracy Letts.** WINNER OF THE 2008 PULITZER PRIZE AND TONY AWARD. When the large Weston family reunites after Dad disappears, their Oklahoma homestead explodes in a maelstrom of repressed truths and unsettling secrets. "Fiercely funny and bitingly sad." *–NY Times.* "Ferociously entertaining." *–Variety.* "A hugely ambitious, highly combustible saga." *–NY Daily News.* [6M, 7W] ISBN: 978-0-8222-2300-9

★ **RUINED by Lynn Nottage.** WINNER OF THE 2009 PULITZER PRIZE. Set in a small mining town in Democratic Republic of Congo, RUINED is a haunting, probing work about the resilience of the human spirit during times of war. "A full-immersion drama of shocking complexity and moral ambiguity." *–Variety.* "Sincere, passionate, courageous." *–Chicago Tribune.* [8M, 4W] ISBN: 978-0-8222-2390-0

★ **GOD OF CARNAGE by Yasmina Reza, translated by Christopher Hampton.** WINNER OF THE 2009 TONY AWARD. A playground altercation between boys brings together their Brooklyn parents, leaving the couples in tatters as the rum flows and tensions explode. "Satisfyingly primitive entertainment." *–NY Times.* "Elegant, acerbic, entertainingly fueled on pure bile." *–Variety.* [2M, 2W] ISBN: 978-0-8222-2399-3

★ **THE SEAFARER by Conor McPherson.** Sharky has returned to Dublin to look after his irascible, aging brother. Old drinking buddies Ivan and Nicky are holed up at the house too, hoping to play some cards. But with the arrival of a stranger from the distant past, the stakes are raised ever higher. "Dark and enthralling Christmas fable." *–NY Times.* "A timeless classic." *–Hollywood Reporter.* [5M] ISBN: 978-0-8222-2284-2

★ **THE NEW CENTURY by Paul Rudnick.** When the playwright is Paul Rudnick, expectations are geared for a play both hilarious and smart, and this provocative and outrageous comedy is no exception. "The one-liners fly like rockets." *–NY Times.* "The funniest playwright around." *–Journal News.* [2M, 3W] ISBN: 978-0-8222-2315-3

★ **SHIPWRECKED! AN ENTERTAINMENT—THE AMAZING ADVENTURES OF LOUIS DE ROUGEMONT (AS TOLD BY HIMSELF) by Donald Margulies.** The amazing story of bravery, survival and celebrity that left nineteenth-century England spellbound. Dare to be whisked away. "A deft, literate narrative." *–LA Times.* "Springs to life like a theatrical pop-up book." *–NY Times.* [2M, 1W] ISBN: 978-0-8222-2341-2